1944-1994

JAGUAR

WORLD WAR II
COMMEMORATIVE COLLECTION

In 1993, Almond & Associates were appointed as
Official Suppliers of Battle of the Atlantic Commemoratives and Souvenirs.
Following on from the great success of this range, which has been supplied to many satisfied customers around the world, we are now proud to present an exclusive selection of items especially designed to commemorate Operation Overlord, that momentous and historic event of World War II that will forever be known as D-Day - Normandy Landings.

D-DAY NORMANDY LANDINGS

REF NO	DESCRIPTION		PRICE
DD 001	T-Shirt, M, L, XL		£ 6.95
DD 001A	T-Shirt, XXL		£ 7.95
DD 002	Sweatshirt, M, L, XL		£12.95
DD 002A	Sweatshirt, XXL		£13.95
DD 003	Baseball Cap		£ 4.95
DD 004	Lapel Badge	22mm	£ 2.95
DD 005	Stick Pin	22mm	£ 2.95
DD 006	Tie Slide	22mm	£ 3.95
DD 007	Cuff Links	22mm	£ 7.45

BATTLE OF THE ATLANTIC

REF NO	DESCRIPTION		PRICE
BA 006A	Fine China Collectors Mug		£ 6.95
BA 033	Lapel Badge	19mm	£ 2.50
BA 034	Stick Pin	19mm	£ 2.50
BA 035	Tie Slide	19mm	£ 3.50
BA 036	Cuff Links	19mm	£ 6.50
BA 037	Atlantic Star Polyester Tie		£ 7.75
BA 037A	Atlantic Star Silk Tie		£19.95
BA 053	Sterling Silver Medal		£29.50
BA 054	Gold Plated Medal		£ 7.95
BA 055	Limited Edition Print		£29.50
BA 056	Fine China 9" Commemorative Plate		£17.50
BA 063A	Stamps - Swordfish & Aircraft Carrier		£ 3.79
BA 063B	Stamps - Liverpool, Washington & Convoy		£ 3.79
BA 063C	Stamps - Atlantic Star Medal & Churchill		£ 3.79

T-Shirts
Navy Blue, 100% Cotton, Badge printed in Red & Gold, Position as shown. Available in M, L, XL and XXL.

Baseball Cap
One size only with back adjuster. Navy Blue, with Badge printed in Red & Gold, position as shown.

Sweatshirts
Navy Blue, soft and comfortable Acrylic/Cotton Fleece. Badge printed in Red & Gold, Position as shown. Available in M, L, XL and XXL.

The Jewellery Collection
Lapel Badge - Gold plated, with Dark Blue & Red Enamel. also available mounted onto Stick Pin, Tie Slide and Cuff Links. (See BA93 range below for comparison)

The Official Commemoration Medal
45mm Hallmarked Sterling Silver Proof Quality Commemorative Medal in Presentation Case, & 45mm Gold Plated Proof Quality Commemorative Medal in Presentation Case. Below: Reverse Side view of medals.

"Shepherding The Flock" BA93 Limited Edition Print 16" x 23" (500 Only)
Signed by well known Liverpool Marine Artist Thomas Shuttleworth, & supplied with a full Certificate of Authenticity and Profile of the Artist.

BA 033 . BA 034 . BA 035 . BA 036

BA 006A . BA 056

BA 053 . BA 054

BA 037 . BA 037A

BA 063A . BA 063B . BA 063C

Please write your order on a separate sheet of paper and attach the completed address slip.
Please check all details and include reference nos. and, where applicable, size, colour etc.
Total your order and add the appropriate postage and packing amount.
Please make Cheques/Postal Orders payable to Almond & Associates.
REMEMBER, on all bulk orders over £100, P&P is FREE!

Name: ....

Address: ....
....

Postcode:..

Tel. No (Daytime) .... (Evening) ....
Please Write Clearly in Block Capitals.

POSTAGE & PACKING
(Please add to your order)

ORDER VALUE	PLEASE ADD*
Up to £5.00	£1.50
Up to 15.00	£3.00
Up to £25.00	£4.50
Up to £50.00	£6.00
Up to £75.00	£8.00
Up to £100	£10.00
Over £100	FREE

U.K Mainland Only. Overseas Customers please enquire P&P rates.

Free Full Colour Catalogue of a wide range of Battle of the Atlantic Souvenirs is available. Please enclose a 25p stamp.   Post your order to:
TRI Service Publications Limited. 62-63, Upper Street, London N1 0NY

D-DAY 50 YEARS ON

CONTENTS

EDITORIAL CHAIRMEN

Colonel Michael Dewar, Maj Gen Julian Thompson,

PUBLISHER *Anthony J. Mullarkey,* **ART DIRECTOR** *Roger Miller*

MARKETING *Loana Vazzano,* **PRODUCTION** *Norman Barnes,*

ADVERTISING MANAGER *Barry Ritchie*

COMPANY CHAIRMAN *Gerald Capps*

50 Years On is published by Tri-Service Publications Ltd.
62 / 63 Upper Street, Islington, London, N1 0NY.
Tel: 071 354 5566. Fax: 071 354 8606.
Repro by BTA Printed by Graphoprint,
Trade Distributors: Seymour, Windsor House, 1270 London Road, SW16 4DH

© 1994 Tri-Service Publications Ltd. 62 / 63 Upper Street, Islington, London, N1 0NY.
Printed in the UK. All rights reserved.
Reproduction in whole or in part without written permission is strictly prohibited.

Cover board printed on Hi - speed Opal Chlorine Free 300gsm, supplied by Arjo Wiggins Fine Papers Ltd.
Many thanks to Colorgraphic - The UK's No.1 Direct Response printer for producing the donation envelopes.

Thanks to:
Imperial War Museum, Lambeth Road, London,

Never was I more proud of the Title 'Master of the Merchant Navy and Fishing Fleets' than at the time of the Normandy Landings, when thousands of Merchant Seamen, in hundreds of ships, took across the channel on that great adventure, our armies and their equipment. Never was pride better justified. This was the greatest combined operation the world has ever seen - perhaps the greatest it will ever see. The three fighting services and the Merchant Navy worked as one vast, complex, but perfectly constructed machine, and won a resounding victory.

Message to The Merchant Navy from King George VI

The Chamber of Shipping
2-5 Minories London EC3N 1BJ
Telephone 071-702 1100
Facsimile 071-626 8135 (Group 3)

MESSAGE
FROM *HM Queen Elizabeth, The Queen Mother*

In June this year we will commemorate the achievements of all those who took part in the D-Day Landings in Normandy. We will remember the men and women of our country and our allies who fought and in some cases gave their lives to provide the foundation for a campaign that would end the war in Europe within a year. I can recall the immense relief and pride felt by all those at home 50 years ago. After four years of war the long hoped for restoration of freedom to France and the world had begun.

As we now celebrate the 50th Anniversary of the D-Day Landings, even those who are too young to recall such memories can appreciate the spirit of vitality and courage required to achieve such a great enterprise.

I am sure this book will provide a fitting commemoration of the events of 50 years ago for both the younger generation and those with personal memories of 1944; and a reminder of what our Armed Services do today.

I send my warmest good wishes to you all.

Elizabeth R

Queen Mother

INTRODUCTION

This book provides a link between Britain's Armed Forces today and their forbears who landed on D-Day 6th June 1944. The first part is devoted to brief descriptions of some of the events of D-Day and the subsequent battle of Normandy. Part two covers, in outline, the roles and tasks of the Armed Forces today. A comprehensive account of every unit, ship and squadron's part in the events of 6th June 1944 and the following weeks is beyond the scope of a short book, and the editors apologise to any of those who took part who feel that undue weight has been given to some participants at the expense of others.

After nearly 50 years of peace in Northwestern Europe, it can be hard, to comprehend the scale of the Invasion of Normandy, and what it meant to the people of the United Kingdom.

By 6th June 1944, the people of these islands had been at war for nearly five years. The assault on Normandy heralded what they hoped was the beginning of the end of their ordeal. The invasion of Northwest Europe was the most stupendous enterprise in the history of warfare.

It changed history, setting the scene for Europe as we know it today. Had it failed, it is possible that the Western Allies might have judged another attempt impossible, for several years at best.

The Americans might have turned their whole attention to the war with Japan. Hitler might have succeeded in stabilising his front with Russia. The Allied armies would not have over-run his V2 rocket bases; with incalculable consequences for Southern England. It is just possible that he would have been left in possession of much of his conquered territory in Western Europe; Norway, France and the Benelux countries.

Planning for the Invasion

Before the arrival in England, in January 1944, of General Dwight D Eisenhower as Supreme Allied commander for the campaign, and General Sir Bernard Montgomery to command 21st Army Group as the overall land force commander, planning for the invasion had been in the hands of the British Lieutenant General Frederick Morgan, Chief of Staff to the Supreme Allied Commander (COSSAC).

Before the long march to the heart of Germany could begin, the assaulting Allies would have to smash through Hitler's Atlantic Wall; stake out enough elbow room into which reinforcing division, supplies and equipment could be landed; and break out.

To breach what Hitler called 'Festung Europe' ('Fortress Europe'), was daunting enough, but having gained a foothold, the only way out of the beachhead lay in defeating the most formidable army in the world,

In Britain, many senior leaders wrestled with fears that it would end in an unparalleled disaster. The spectre of the bloody battles of attrition on the Western Front 1914-1918 hung over Churchill. Even that master of strategy, the Chief of the Imperial General Staff, Field Marshal Sir Alan Brooke, said to Morgan, having outlined the resources available, "Well, there it is. It won't work, but you must bloody well make it".

The first question faced by the planners was where to land. Morgan's answer was Normandy. He and his staff had arrived at this by starting with the requirement for unchallenged air superiority over the beachhead. The radius of action of the most numerous Allied fighters, Spitfires flying from bases in southern England, ruled out anywhere west of the Cotentin Peninsula, and east of the Pas de Calais. By a process of elimination, only two possible beachheads were deemed suitable: the Pas de Calais, and the coast of Normandy between the River Seine and the eastern side of the Cotentin Peninsula.

The Pas de Calais was close to the English coast, and would therefore enable Allied fighters more time on station over the beachhead, and shipping a quicker turn-around. Furthermore, it lay on the shortest route to the heart of Germany.

For these reasons, the planners assessed that the Germans would expect an attack in this area. The most formidable defences along the Atlantic Wall were sited in the Pas de Calais; an indication that the Germans agreed with the Allied

planners' assessment. A major disadvantage of the Normandy option was the lack of ports. Both Cherbourg and Le Havre were outside the area selected for the initial lodgement, and the Germans would undoubtedly fight hard to deny them to the Allies. The ingenious Mulberry, artificial harbours were the Allied answer to the problem.

From the moment of his arrival to take command of 21 Army Group, Montgomery's leadership was crucial to the success of the operation. He endorsed the selection of the area for landing, but vehemently opposed the COSSAC plan for the assault, which envisaged an initial landing by three divisions aimed at capturing Caen, followed by over-ambitious simultaneous thrusts to Cherbourg, Brittany and Paris.

The Allies were fortunate that Montgomery, with full backing from Eisenhower changed the plan. With the advantage of hindsight, the COSSAC plan would have ended in disaster. The Germans would have 'roped off' the limited beachhead envisaged. If the five seaborne divisions that eventually landed could not reach their D-Day objectives, three would have had even less chance of success. The Allied rate of build-up would have never matched, let alone overtaken that of the Germans.

It is easy from the vantage point of 50 years to be over-critical of General Morgan, but he and his staff determined many of the basic considerations that would produce success, including the all important selection of the beachhead. What they lacked was dynamic leadership, backed up by up-to-date battle experience. This Montgomery provided.

His total professionalism, clarity of thought, and confidence in the outcome, was breath of fresh air, which affected everybody from Churchill down to the youngest soldier.

Within less than three weeks of being appointed, Montgomery proposed landing five seaborne divisions in the leading waves, two American, two British and one Canadian. Landings by two airborne brigades envisaged in the COSSAC plan, were expanded to three airborne divisions.

An Allied Effort

Without the massive United States contribution, both in materiel and manpower, there would have been no question of invading Northwest Europe. Neither must we forget the contribution to victory by French, Norwegian, Polish, Belgian, Dutch and Czechoslovak forces. But the invasion and subsequent fighting in Northwest Europe also represented a supreme effort on the part of the British and Canadian people. Of the 156,000 troops landed by sea and air on D-Day, some 84,000 were British and Canadian. Nearly 80 per cent of the naval support was British and Canadian, and half the vast air armada. The sea, land and air commanders-in-chief under General Eisenhower were British. Of course as the campaign progressed, the Americans greatly outnumbered their allies, eventually putting five armies into the field, to one each from Britain, Canada and France.

The Navies and Air Forces

The popular image of soldiers wading ashore in Normandy, tends to overshadow the contribution made by the Allied

navies and air forces. Up to 6th June 1944, the Royal Navy and Royal Air Force, had borne the major burden of the British part in the war, without respite since 1939.

Had the Battle of the Atlantic not been won, in which in the Royal and Canadian Navies played a leading role, with indispensable support from Royal Air Force Coastal Command, all plans for assaulting Normandy would have been academic. The Battle of the Atlantic began in September 1939 and finished on 8th May 1945 with the surrender of Germany.

One of the effect of the strategic bombing campaign by RAF Bomber Command and the US 8th Air Force, was to force the Luftwaffe into concentrating most of its effort into defending Germany. As a result, 2nd Tactical Air Force and 9th US Air Force had little competition in the skies over Normandy.

The Luftwaffe hardly appeared in daylight, and were reduced to nuisance raids by night. The part played by the tactical air forces in support of ground forces in Normandy and throughout the campaign, was a key ingredient in the Allied victory.

The soldiers owed much to Air Marshal Sir Trafford Leigh-Mallory, the Commander-in-Chief Allied Expeditionary Air Force. His plan for destroying the German communication net-work to the Normandy battle front, mainly the French railways, was also a major contribution to the Allied success.

The safe and timely arrival of the armies off the coast of Normandy lay in the hands of the Allied navies, covered by the air forces. Success depended on a host of factors: skillful staff work, joint training and rehearsals, sailing and assembling a mass of shipping, navigating through swept lanes, disembarking on the correct beaches; escorts, bombardment, the turn-round of craft.

All this and much more was the responsibility of Admiral Sir Bertram Ramsay, the Allied Naval Commander. The maritime tasks did not end on D-Day. The break-out of the Allied armies depended on a massive build-up of troops, tanks, guns, ammunition, fuel, and thousands of tons of other supplies and equipment landed over open beaches.

During the first six days of the operation, 326,547 men, 54,186 vehicles and 104,428 tons of stores were landed over these beaches. Later, vast quantities were unloaded through the two artificial Mulberry harbours, each larger than Dover. But even these were vulnerable to weather, as the great gale in mid-June was to demonstrate.

The Essential role of the Russians

Despite massive Allied naval and air supremacy, there would have been no question on invading, and sustaining a land campaign in, Northwest Europe had it not been for the Russians. From 1941 to May 1945, the Red Army engaged the major part of the German Army in one of the bloodiest campaigns in history. On 6 June, over 200 German divisions were deployed on the Eastern Front, leaving some 60 confronting the Allies in the West. The USSR lost over 11 million dead and missing in battle, and six million prisoners. The Battle of Berlin alone, from 16th April to 8th may 1945 cost the Red Army 305,000 casualties.

The Approach of D-Day

In late May and early June, troops moved into sealed transit camps, and were either briefed here, or after embarkation. After a 24-hour postponement because of adverse weather, the vast armarda set sail, from ports in the United Kingdom, from Oban right round to the Forth. An officer with one of the Commandos remembered:

All the shipping was quietly and slowly filling out through the booms, the LCTs with their camouflaged loads of tanks and ammunition, the big LSTs packed with vehicles, the LSIs, all slung around with their LCAs, and the little LCIs with their troops sardined aboard. Besides all these hundreds of craft, were countless corvettes and frigates, rows of destroyers, cruisers and the monitor Roberts. It was wonderful to watch the quiet steady stream of craft slipping out past the Portsmouth forts, so silent and orderly, with no sirens or fuss.

That evening allied airborne troops were also moving to airfields to emplane in aircraft of gliders. The die was cast.

D-Day

Soon after midnight on 6th June 1944, the British 6th Airborne Division landed by parachute and gliders east of the River Orne and the Caen Canal, and the United States 82nd and 101st Airborne Divisions likewise, north and north-west of Carentan, at the base of the Cotentin Peninsular. Their tasks were to protect the flanks of the beachhead, silence selected German batteries and strongpoints, and seize key bridges and routes.

Soon after dawn the seaborne assault began, preceded by a massive sea and air bombardment. In the west, Lieutenant-General Omar Bradley's US 1st Army landed on Utah and Omaha Beaches. In the centre and east, Lieutenant-General Sir Miles Dempsey's British 2nd Army landed on Gold, Juno and Sword Beaches. The British landings were spearheaded by special assault teams of Major General Hobart's 79th Armoured Division, combat engineers in Armoured Vehicles Royal Engineers (AVRE), and swimming tanks.

By nightfall the Allies had gained a foothold on the Continent of Europe. Surprise had been achieved, the troops had fought with spirit and determination. all assaulting divisions were ashore, although not all D-Day objectives had been taken. There were still gaps between the British 2nd Army, US Vth Corps and US VIIth Corps.

There were pockets of enemy resistance to be mopped up within all beachhead areas.

There was a dangerous salient at Douvres between the Canadians and British I Corps. Fortunately the German reaction had been slow and uncoordinated. Only 21st Panzer Division had attacked that day, and the Douvres salient was the result. But there were reports that other German divisions would soon join in the effort to rope-off the Allies and push them back into the sea. The Allied efforts for the next few days were directed at linking up the beachheads, and expanding the lodgement area.

Once the armies had built up their strengths ashore, Montgomery's strategy was to draw the bulk of the German armour on to his left flank, to allow the Americans on the right to capture Cherbourg, and then break out in a wide turning movement.

He accepted that the burden of the grinding battles necessary to keep the Panzer divisions pulled in on his left would be borne by the British, Canadians, and latterly the Poles. He adhered unwaveringly to this strategy despite criticism from other senior Allied commanders, and was vindicated when the Allied armies, having broken out, crossed the River Seine ahead of the forecast date.

D-Day
at the National Army Museum

18 May to 18 September 1994

Rex Whistler's War

A Special Exhibition to mark the the fiftieth anniversary of the death of the artist, Rex Whistler, who was killed in July 1944 whilst serving with the Welsh Guards in Normandy.

In addition to his well-known theatre designs and book illustrations, the Exhibition shows some of Whistler's portraits, landscapes, and amusing paintings intended to enliven drab army barracks.

Monty's Men: The British Soldier and the D-Day Campaign.

An Exhibition which concentrates on the experiences of the individual soldier rather than on strategic issues. It examines the things of importance to 'Monty's men', such as what they ate, how they slept and what it was like to be a soldier in combat during this decisive campaign.

Admission Free

NATIONAL ARMY MUSEUM CHELSEA

The National Army Museum, Royal Hospital Road, Chelsea, London SW3 4HT

Open daily 10.00am to 5.30pm.

THE NATION UNDER ARMS

By the time General Dwight Eisenhower took up his post as

supreme Commander Allied Expeditionary Force in January 1944,

the British people and the British economy had been

mobilised for war purposes to a greater degree than any

other belligerent nation, Allied or enemy.

No less than 55 per cent of the manpower resources of the coun-

try were in the armed forces, the civil defence services

or in civilian war employment. The comparable figure for the

United States was only 40 per cent. The number of women in

work had risen in Britain by 10 per cent over peacetime;

in America by only six per cent.

Half of these British women were directly serving the war effort. Much to the resentment of male craftsmen and their unions, they now operated the new American machine-tools in the factories; they assembled the Spitfires and the Lancasters.

Opposite
Women workers attaching the skin of an aircraft to its frame.

In civilian uniform they nursed, drove ambulances and served in civil defence; they crewed the buses, trams and trains; or in the Women's Land Army replaced the farm workers who had gone to war, so contributing greatly to the doubling of the output of British farms during the war.

In the armed services women (including Princess Elizabeth, now Queen Elizabeth II) drove the motor transport and maintained it in the workshops; they crewed (like Mary Churchill, daughter of the Prime Minister, now Lady Soames) anti-aircraft batteries; they staffed the operations rooms of the Royal Navy and Royal Air Force, and piloted aircraft for RAF Transport Command. All in all, the traditional stereotype of the homebound 'little woman' proved one of the major casualties of the war.

It serves as another measure of Britain's effort that whereas the American national income actually rose during the war, the British were reduced by strict rationing and empty shops to an austerity the gloom of which was deepened by five years of blackout.

All in all, by 1944 Great Britain had become a specialised warrior state, its economy only kept afloat by American supplies under Lend-Lease.

As a result of this total mobilisation, British aircraft factories would turn out in 1944 nearly 25,000 aircraft, 2,400 of them in the month of OVERLORD alone. By that month wartime output of tanks had reached a cumulative total of 25,000. Of special relevance to Operation NEPTUNE (the naval side of OVERLORD), British yards turned out nearly 160,000 tons of warships from January to June 1944, plus 700,000 tons of landing-ships and landing-craft.

Yet there was a darker side to these impressive production achievements. In the coal industry, the nation's key energy source, two million tons of production were lost through strikes in the first quarter of 1944 alone.

In shipbuilding 'who-does-what' demarkation disputes between the unions, coupled in some yards with cramped layouts and obsolete equipment, held back output. Even the aircraft industry witnessed wild-cat local strikes, disrupting production.

Moreover, the backbone of the British armoured divisions in OVERLORD would be the American Sherman tank, while the mobility of all British divisions would depend largely on trucks and jeeps made in North America.

On a Britain already stretched to the limit there fell between January and June 1944 the huge task of acting as the launching base for the greatest amphibious operation in history. The woods, commons and parks of southern England were filled with tanks, motor transport and supply dumps - with camps and training areas to accommodate the 37 divisions allotted to the Normandy campaign.

For the local people it meant further upset in their difficult wartime lives, even in some cases evacuation.

The construction industry worked flat-out to complete all the 'hards' needed for landing craft in the little harbours from Yarmouth in the east round to Falmouth in the west, and to build repair shops, amphibious bases and training centres, especially for the American navy and army.

Yet preparations for OVERLORD also laid particular technological loads on Britain's hard-pressed war economy. To the problem of supplying the armies in Normandy with abundant petrol an ingenious answer had been found in Pluto - 'Pipeline Under the Ocean', or, rather, across the bed of the English Channel. The two types of pipe adopted for PLUTO called for 15,000 tons of steel and 6,000 tons of lead alloy respectively, as well as specially-adapted craft for unrolling the pipes into the sea, and the pumps, pumping houses and other gear for the terminal at the English end. But the largest single construction feat lay in the components of the two

ARMSCOR SALUTES THE BRAVE, THE BOLD, AND THE INNOVATIVE.

South Africa is proud to be counted amongst the brave who broke the iron grip of World War 2. Armscor pays tribute to the courageous men involved in this triumphant operation, those they left behind and the many others who will never forget 6 June 1944.

In training over 33 000 allied airmen during World War 2, South Africa made an enormous contribution to peace in the world. Today, 50 years later, we add machine force to human mastery through the South African Armaments industry, which is uniquely developed to play an important role internationally.

It couldn't be made better value.

So we just build it better.

When the Volkswagen Group bought Skoda, they bought a car maker with unequalled reputation for value for money. No-one has ever made cars that gave you more for the price.

And now Skoda uses the same quality standards as the rest of the Volkswagen Group.

In only a couple of years, Volkswagen has revolutionised the way Skoda cars are built.

The materials we use, our working practices and perhaps most importantly, the way our cars are tested.

Skoda has learnt a great deal about quality from Volkswagen.

But when it comes to offering value for money, there is no one who has anything to teach Skoda.

The Favorit range of 5 door hatchbacks and estates costs from only **£5,574**' 'on the road' including all delivery charges, number plates, VAT, six months road tax and an unlimited mileage warranty with AA 'emergency' cover for two years.

Phone free on **0500 34 44 54** for more information and where to find your local Skoda Dealer.

The new Skoda
Volkswagen Group

*Prices correct at time of going to press. Model illustrated Favorit Estate GLXiE at £7,446 'on the road'. UK Mainland only.

Right
Saddle of a 25 pounder gun being welded by Miriam Higgins.
Below
Women brick - layers.

MULBERRY artificial harbours, on which the supply and build-up of the Allied armies in Normandy would critically depend, and which were to be towed across the Channel and put in place on the French coast by D + 18. The MULBER-RIES comprised 400 different units totalling 1.5 million tons. The 'Phoenix' concrete caissons to form the main breakwaters were themselves each 400 feet long and displaced up to 6,000 tons.

Ninety thousand tons of scarce steel were required for the floating 'Bombardons' of the outer breakwaters, together with the 23 floating pierheads and 10 miles of floating piers. All in all, 45,000 men had to be found at a time of supreme shortage of labour to fabricate all the complex components of the Mulberries. The problem was worse in the case of skilled men, for the Phoenix caissons demanded 1,200 scaffolders, more than the total available supply in the country, while welders and steel erectors to make the components for the floating piers were equally hard to find.

That the Mulberry components were ready on schedule to be towed or carried to the Normandy shore is a signal tribute to the resourcefulness of the British war economy under pressure.

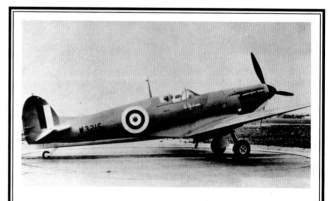

Amid the daily problems of wartime life - bombing, blackouts, rationing and shortages - Marks and Spencer staff found time to knit thousands of garments for the Forces, to collect for a presentation to the nation of a spitfire aircraft aptly named *The Marksman*, and to organize emergancy canteens for dockyard workers, bombed - refugees and servicemen on leave as well as sharing their staff canteens with evacuee children.

MARKS & SPENCER

We give thanks for the legacy of D-Day.

THE RUN-UP TO D-DAY

THE COMMANDERS

On 15 May 1944 King George VI and Prime Minister Winston Churchill attended a full-scale briefing on the invasion plans at St Paul's School in West London. They were taken through the details by members of a command team that had been established earlier in the year.

Known as Supreme Headquarters Allied Expeditionary Force (SHAEF), it was led by US General Dwight D Eisenhower, moved from command of Allied forces in the Mediterranean where he had gained a deserved reputation for planning skill and inter-Allied co-operation.

His deputy for OVERLORD was Air Chief Marshal Sir Arthur Tedder, who had been his deputy in the Mediterranean and was well versed in the intricacies of ground-air co-ordination.

Air Chief Marshal Sir Trafford Leigh-Mallory was given command of the Allied air forces for the invasion and

Admiral Sir Bertram Ramsay commanded the naval forces.

General Sir Bernard Montgomery, the hero of Alamein, was to command the ground forces during the invasion and subsequent breakout, with Lieutenant-General Omar N Bradley and Lieutenant-General Sir Miles Dempsey in charge of the main assault formations - the US First and British Second Armies respectively. Major-General Walter Bedell Smith, a long-time associate of Eisenhower's, was appointed Chief of Staff, again continuing a relationship forged in the Mediterranean.

*The Allied command team for D-Day and the Battle for Normandy: **Front Row (left to right)** Air Chief Marshal Sir Arthur Tedder (Deputy Supreme Commander), General Dwight D Eisenhower (Supreme Commander, General Sir Bernard Montgomery (Commander 21st Army Group and overall land commander). **Back Row (left to right)** Lieutenant General Omar N Bradley (Commander United States 1st Army for the invasion and subsequently United States 12th Army Group), Admiral Sir Bertram Ramsay (C-in-C Allied Naval Forces), Air Chief Marsal Sir Trafford Leigh-Mallory (C-in-C Allied Expeditionary Air Forces), Lieutenant General Walter Bedell Smith (Chief of Staff Supreme Headquarters Allied Expeditionary Force)*

At the St Paul's School briefing, it was decided that D-Day for the invasion would be set at 5th June, with Y-Day, the day by which all preparations would be complete on 1st June. By then, the assault troops were packed into closed camps along the south coast of England, the Americans in Devon and Dorset opposite the planned US landing area, the British and Canadians further east in Sussex and Hampshire. Final briefings were given to the soldiers at the end of May. The weather was good, with all the clarity and freshness of an early British summer.

It was not destined to last. Early on 4th June SHAEF meteorologists, led by RAF Group Captain James Stagg, presented a worrying weather picture to Eisenhower. A gale, the worst for 20 years, was about to move into the English Channel, bringing low cloud that would ground the air forces and rough seas that would disrupt the invasion fleet.

Eisenhower had no choice but to postpone the operation for 24 hours, recalling some of the ships that had already set sail. At 0930 hours on 4th June, Stagg presented a slightly more optimistic forecast: the weather was likely to clear during the night of 5th/6th June and remain so during the morning of the 6th, before closing in again.

Eisenhower consulted his team: Leigh-Mallory was not keen, but Montgomery and Ramsay both wanted to go ahead. It was left to Eisenhower. After a long silence, he spoke: 'I am quite positive we must give the order ... I don't like it, but there it is'.

A final meeting was held at 0400 hours on 5th June. The forecast was still favourable and Eisenhower finally committed the Allies to the assault on 6th June. 'OK', he said, 'Let's go' !

BEACH RECONNAISSANCE

Choosing the beaches for the landings was a complex matter. They had to be within reach of the massive airpower now deployed in Britain, and in reasonable sailing time from British waters. The invasion site had to offer a direct route into the heart of occupied Europe. The beaches of both Normandy and the Pas de Calais had their advantages at this grand strategic level.

But the characteristics of the beaches themselves were important too. The approaches to them should be comparatively clear of rocks and shoals. The beach gradients should be neither so steep that disembarking amphibious vehicles would find it difficult to climb them, nor so shallow that landing craft would 'take the ground' so far out as to expose disembarking troops to a long period of enemy fire without cover. The quality of the sand itself was vital. Above all, it must be firm enough to take tanks. Finally, the beaches should have good exits, allowing rapid consolidation and providing room for the thousands of reinforcements necessary to defend the beachhead against the expected counter-attack of German reserves.

Bitter experience had shown that normal peace-time charts were not accurate enough for such fine but crucial calculations. Local intelligence, low flying aircraft taking photographs and reconnaissance from the periscope of a submarine lurking a mile of so offshore helped a good deal, but none of these provided enough information unless the beaches were inspected and examined in person, if necessary right under the noses of the defenders.

For this reason, the Chief of Combined Operations set up 'Combined Operations Pilotage Parties' which reconnoitred all the possible beaches of Normandy and the Pas de Calais. Inevitably, some parties never returned from their highly dangerous and demanding work, but the information they provided swayed the Allies into choosing Normandy rather than the Pas de Calais and almost certainly saved many thousands of allied lives when the invasion eventually took place.

Disturbingly, the Germans began to build underwater obstacles in the landing area from February 1944. Channel tides have a rise and fall of up to 20 feet and at low water a long foreshore of rather more than 500 yards is exposed. The Germans assumed that the Allies would prefer to land at or near high tide [to reduce the width of beach to be crossed] and so began to construct formidable obstacles on the foreshore, that would be underwater at high tide. This meant they would be in the best position to rip the bottom out of the landing craft with their precious cargoes, as they neared the beaches. There was one obstacle every two to three yards and the Germans were obviously working their way down to the low-water line. The obstacles themselves were ferocious constructions weighing a ton and more, and liberally bedecked with mines. Small interservice parties went regularly ashore to investigate these defences, accumulating as much information as they could to help the clearance teams who would clearly have to accompany, and indeed precede the main invasion force.

PRE D-DAY ATTACKS ON RAIL AND OTHER TARGETS

The Royal Air Force's direct contribution to D-Day commenced on 9th February 1944 when medium bombers of No. 2 Group made the first of a series of raids against the French railway system.

The aim of the Allied Transportation Plan was the dislocation of the French and Belgian road and rail system to delay German reinforcements from reaching Normandy in the critical days after the invasion.

Whilst the smaller targets such as bridges and rolling stock could be tackled by the fighters and medium bombers of the Allied Expeditionary Air Forces, larger targets, including the all-important marshalling yards and major rail junctions, required the efforts of RAF Bomber Command.

By June 1944 Bomber Command could field a force of 82 squadrons operating over 1,600 bombers. The main force consisted of five groups of Lancasters and Halifaxes which were supported by the Pathfinders of No. 8 Group and the radio and radar countermeasures squadrons of No. 100 Group. It must be remembered that the United States 8th Army Air Force also played a major part in the pre-invasion bombing campaign by flying daylight raids on similar targets to Bomber Command.

Allied attacks on the rail network increased in ferocity as D-Day approached. During March Bomber Command made nine raids on rail targets, April saw 22 raids and during May

RAF to the preparation for D-Day. Despite Allied gains, the German submarine force concentrated in the Bay of Biscay and Norwegian ports still posed a serious threat to the invasion fleet. To seal off the English Channel for the invasion forces to operate freely, Coastal Command mounted a major anti-submarine effort from April which resulted in a major defeat for the U-boat fleet. German light surface craft, mostly E-boats, were the target of Coastal Command's Beaufighter squadrons.

During the period between 1st April and D-Day itself the RAF flew almost 72,000 sorties and dropped 94,000 tons of bombs, almost half of which were aimed at the railway system. The success of the pre-invasion bombing together with the post-invasion campaign caused the Germans sever logistics problems in reinforcing and resupplying their forces in Normandy and contributed in no small measure to the success of OPERATION OVERLORD.

Left
Vire Railways yards after bombing.
Below
Engine after bombing by Allied Air Forces.

and the first week of June another 32 raids were made. A total of 160 bombers were lost during the course of these raids, all of which were made at night.

The assault on the railway system resulted in major disruption to the German line of communications which had a long-term effect on their ability to counter the Allied offensive.

During May Bomber Command increased its target coverage to include coastal gun batteries which were difficult targets as they were small (from an airman's point of view) and usually embedded in thick concrete. Coastal radar and signal stations were also bombed as D-Day approached and Luftwaffe airfields were attacked by the heavy bombers as well as by tactical aircraft. During this time Bomber Command also maintained its attack on German strategic centres as well as bombing V-1 flying bomb sites which were then posing a major threat. The bombing of transportation and other targets was carefully chosen to give the Germans the impression that the Pas de Calais area was the location chosen for the invasion whilst still achieving the aim of isolating Normandy by 6th June.

The pre-invasion bombing campaign was by no means the only contribution made by the

Remember the events of June 194

BT is pleased to have produced four limited edition £2 Phonecards in honour of the 50th Anniversary of D-Day. Featuring images from the Imp

arry a photograph in your wallet.

Museum collection, they're on sale from May 9th – for three weeks only – from most BT Phonecard stockists.

We go further, to bring you closer

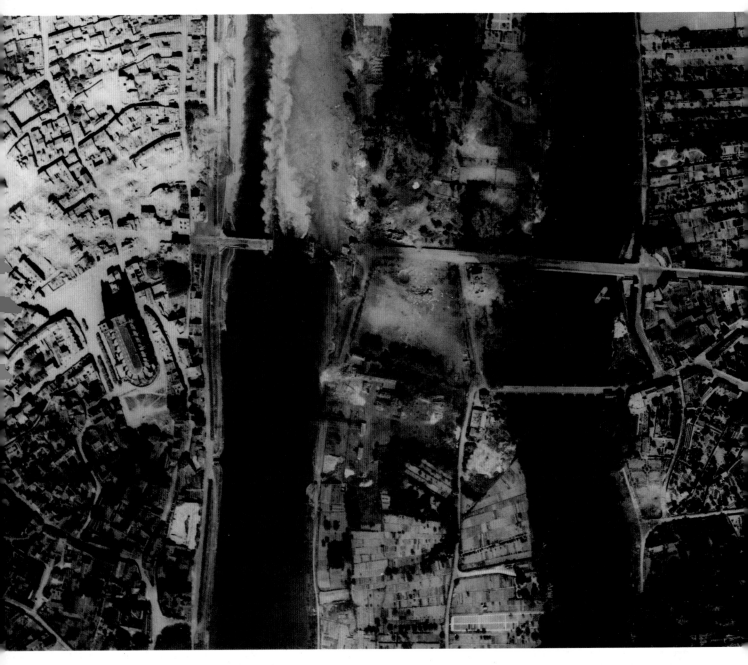

THE AIR OFFENSIVE

Although RAF transport aircraft and gliders were amongst the first Allied aircraft over Normandy in the early hours of 6th June, it fell to Bomber Command to open large-scale offensive air operations on D-Day. Bomber Command's efforts can be divided into two distinct categories: bombing raids against coastal batteries; and deception operations using an array of electronic countermeasures and other techniques.

Ten coast batteries (five in the British sector and five in the American sector) were allocated as targets for Bomber Command which planned a maximum-effort attack under the code name OPERATION FLASHLAMP. Three batteries were attacked early in the night to assist their capture by the airborne forces but the other targets were not hit until just before dawn in order for the naval bombardment to then take over and maintain a continuous rain of fire on the coastal positions. Pathfinder aircraft marked the targets and a total of

1,056 Lancasters, Halifaxes and Mosquitoes attacked dropping 5,267 tons of bombs, an average of approximately 500 tons on each target. Several of the batteries had been attacked in the months preceding D-Day with the unfortunate consequence that some of the guns had been moved to new positions. Damage assessment was difficult because the targets were later attacked by medium bombers and fighter-bombers as well as by naval bombardment, but it was noted that the 500 and 1,000 lb bombs had made little impact on the thick concrete roofs which protected most batteries. However, even if the guns were not actually destroyed by Bomber Command's attacks, they had at least been silenced during the critical period when the invasion fleet first came within range and the attacks, the heaviest air raids during a single day up to that date, had thereby achieved their aim and had done so for the loss of only six aircraft.

In comparison with OPERATION FLASHLAMP, the radio counter-measures effort involved much smaller Bomber

Command forces but were still of enormous importance to the success of Overlord. The twin aims of the Radio Counter-Measures Plan was to deceive the Germans into believing that the invasion was about to take place in the Pas de Calais area whilst at the same time protecting the real invasion forces during the voyage to Normandy.

In conjunction with naval deception efforts, Lancasters of No. 617 Squadron and Stirlings of No. 218 Squadron dropped a dense screen of metallic foil known as Window in a precise and slowly advancing pattern across the English Channel. On the German radars this screen looked like a large convoy approaching the Pas de Calais area. OPERATION TITANIC involved Halifaxes and Stirlings carrying out further deception operations by dropping miniature dummy parachutists and pyrotechnic devices to simulate airborne assaults near Rouen, Maltot and Marigny far away form the actual landings.

The specially-equipped Lancasters of No. 101 Squadron which carried German-speaking radio operators successfully confused the German night fighter system by jamming radio transmissions. The Lancasters drew most of the night fighters which got airborne, lost one aircraft, and claimed a kill for themselves. German early-warning radar was successfully jammed by Stirlings of No. 199 Squadron which orbited over the Channel for most of the night providing a screen behind which the bombers and transports flew towards Normandy undetected. Mosquito intruders and night fighters from No. 100 Group and Air Defence of Great Britain (ADGB) flew patrols over France and the Low Countries to intercept German night fighters attempting to make their way to Normandy.

On the morning of 6th June daylight air operations over Normandy became the responsibility of the Allied Expeditionary Air Forces. This was the joint British and American organisation established for the invasion of Europe and which consisted of a vast armada of some 300 squadrons capable of putting up over 6,000 tactical aircraft. Precise command and control of such a vast armada of air power was critical and a Combined Operations Room was set up at Hillingdon to oversee the tactical air operations, both offensive and defensive, involving British and American forces.

The RAF was responsibe for night air defence of the invasion forces, whilst the 2nd Tactical Air Force and the US 9th Air Force was responsible for daylight cover over Normandy. During daylight hours a rotation of six squadrons of Spitfires were on standing patrol over the beachhead continuously, while other aircraft escorted transports and bombers to and from Normandy. The Spitfires were fitted with extra fuel tanks to give them 50 minutes more over the assault area before returning to base. As an indication of the international Allied effort on D-Day it is interesting to note that of the 36 Spitfire squadrons which provided this airborne umbrella, ten squadrons were Canadian, four French, four Polish, three Czech, two Norwegian, two Belgian, one Australian, one New Zealand; in addition to nine regular and auxiliary RAF squadrons. These squadrons were backed up by a further 15

Spitfire, Mustang and Tempest squadrons which acted as a ready reserve and the Mustang wings provided escort to Coastal Command strikes and the airborne forces during OPERATION MALLARD.

Following on the work of Bomber Command, the Allied Expeditionary Air Force (AEAF) continued the isolation of Normandy by bombing bridges, road junctions and, to a lesser extent, rail targets. This task fell largely to the Mosquitos and Mitchells of No. 2 Group, which started their work during the evening of 5th June and continued until just after dawn. No. 2 Group's two Boston squadrons (Nos. 88 and 343 - Free French) had the task of laying a smoke screen to protect the invasion fleet from the heavy gun batteries at Le Havre and Cap Barfluer.

Close air support for the soldiers was provided by eighteen Typhoon squadrons on D-Day. Eleven squadrons were armed with rocket projectiles with the remaining seven armed with 500 lb bombs Twelve of the squadrons flew their first sorties against pre-arranged targets including strong points on or just behind the beaches, batteries, barracks and other military targets near the coast. The "cab rank" system was used in which immediate strikes could be called for by troops on the ground. A few requests from the army and navy for attacks on strongpoints were successfully accomplished, but generally the complete surprise which the Germans experienced on D-Day resulted in a slow reaction with little movement on the roads behind the beach head, and consequently few targets for the Typhoon squadrons held in reserve for this type of target. Later in the day the Typhoons were allowed to range further inland to find worthwhile targets, and in doing so met with some of the few Luftwaffe fighters encountered during D-Day. Several of the Typhoon squadrons flew three missions during the day, and a total of 400 sorties were flown by typhoons for the loss of eight aircraft.

Throughout the day the Combined Operations Room were kept informed of events and in particular enemy movements by the tactical and photographic reconnaissance squadrons of the AEAF. The five Mustang tactical reconnaissance squadrons had a very busy day but many photographic sorties were spoilt by low cloud. RAF Mustang and Spitfire squadrons also formed part of the Air Spotting Pool which flew continuously throughout the day providing target information to the bombardment ships.

By 2000 hours on D-Day the AEAF had flown no less than 3,796 sorties for the loss of 30 aircraft, mostly from flak. The fighter squadrons maintained a constant vigil over the beaches and the approaches to Normandy, but such was the success of the various deception plans, the isolation of Northern France by intruders and ADGB aircraft and the POINTBLANK counter-air campaign, that the Luftwaffe was unable to mount a major effort over Normandy. Several attempts were made by units of Luftflotte 3 to intercept Allied bombers and ground attack aircraft, but most were engaged by the protective screen of RAF and USAAF fighters. By the end of the day the Luftwaffe had lost 31 aircraft with a further seven damaged. Late in the evening a growing concentration of enemy armour was noted south of Caen and No. 2 Group's bombers were asked to attack bridges, road junctions and traffic in this area thus bringing to a close the RAF's participation in the busiest and perhaps most historic day of the war.

D-DAY DECEPTION PLANNING

OPERATION BODYGUARD

By early 1944 nobody needed convincing that deception operations paid off. Even the Americans, who had initially regarded deception as an unnecessary subtlety in view of their superior mobility, firepower and material resources, had come round to the idea. They entered wholeheartedly into the most ambitious deception plan in the history of warfare - the plan to protect OVERLORD, the Allied invasion of France in June 1944, codenamed Operation BODYGUARD.

The Allied deception planners already had an advantage in knowing (from signals intelligence gained from the ULTRA code-breakers at Bletchley whose activities revealed so much about German strategic thinking) that Hitler had already arrived at the conclusion that the main Allied onslaught would come across the Straits of Dover. This was endorsed by Field Marshals von Runstedt and Rommel and Admiral Krancke, the Commanders who would have to face the Allied invasion. It certainly was the most logical choice: the sea crossing was the shortest possible where the turnaround of landing craft and the building of the beachhead would be the quickest. The short flight time from airfields in the south of England would allow aircraft to maximise their time over the battle area. It was the shortest route to the main Allied objective - the heartland of Germany. It would ensure the destruction of the V1 V2 and V3 sites in the Pas de Calais (the V3 was the large cross channel gun, the Hochdruckpumpe, located at Calais - Mimoyeques). And, of course, it provided at least one major port. Bearing all this in mind, Hitler had garrisoned the Pas de Calais with the German 15th Army, the strongest force in the West.

The BODYGUARD deception plans were confined to an organisation known as the London Controlling Section (LCS) consisting of two naval officers, an RAF officer and five army officers operating in extreme secrecy in Churchill's underground headquarters in the Mall. The LCS maintained close liaison with the combined Chiefs of Staff and the Operations staff of Supreme Headquarters, Allied Expeditionary Force (SHAEF) who put the deception plans into effect. The LCS decided, with Churchill's approval, that the essentials of the deception story that would be fed to Hitler and his chief intelligence officer in the West, Colonel Baron von Roenne, would be:

That land operations in 1944 would begin in the spring with a combined British, American and Russian attack on Norway followed by a move into Sweden and subsequently Denmark and North Germany.

That the main Allied effort in 1944 would be in the Balkans. This would consist of an Allied invasion of the Peloponnese and an advance into South Germany through the Ljubljana Gap coordinated with a Russian attack to gain the Ploesti oilfields which provided Hitler with a third of his supplies. That, if the Allies were to invade France at all in 1944, it could not be before July.

That, when the invasion of France did come, it would be directed against the Pas de Calais area.

That the ground forces for an invasion of Norway, for the main attack across the straits of Dover and for diversionary landings elsewhere in France were fully equipped, trained and standing by in Britain whilst follow-up divisions were ready to move from America.

In addition, the BODYGUARD planners would have to encourage the belief that the landings on the coast of Normandy, when they did occur, were only a diversion designed to draw the 15th Army away from the Pas de Calais. Similarly, they must prevent any move north into Normandy of the German 21st Army soon after the D-Day landings.

There was no single overall plan for BODYGUARD because the scale of it would have been so immense and the design so complex as to render it unworkable. Rather, it was decided to develop separate plans for specific geographical areas. These plans were again so complex that they had to be broken down into subsidiary schemes which had their own codenames. The main component parts of the BODYGUARD Operation were codenamed FORTITUDE, ZEPPELIN, VENDETTA and IRONSIDE.

FORTITUDE was the codename given to the deception plan to convince Hitler that a massive attack would take place on the Pas de Calais as well as an Allied landing in Norway. There were two sub-divisions of FORTITUDE. The first, FORTITUDE NORTH, was concerned with the fictitious invasion of Norway, the bringing of Sweden into the war on the side of the Allies and the subsequent invasion of North Germany through Denmark. The threat to Norway was posed by the non-existent British 4th Army with its headquarters in Edinburgh Castle and its two constituent formations, the 2nd (British) Corps and 7th (British) Corps, located in Stirling and Dundee respectively. This entire charade was fabricated by Colonel McLeod and a small band of radio operators who simulated the radio transmissions of these formations. The presence of the British 4th Army was also made known to the Germans through leaks to double agents, references in BBC broadcasts and publicity in local and national newspapers. These reported sporting fixtures between non-existent units and formations, engagements and marriages between locals and soldiers serving in these units and even published letters from the same non-existent soldiers. Colonel McLeod was particularly pleased when the Germans tried to bomb his Army HQ.

Perhaps the most successful aspect of FORTITUDE NORTH was the mission of Air Vice-Marshal Thornton, the pre-war Air Attache in Stockholm, to the Commander-in-Chief of the Swedish Air Force, General Nordenskjold, with whom he had been on particularly good terms, to sound out the Swedish reaction to the proposed Allied invasion of Norway. Thornton duly flew to Stockholm in civilian clothes and was whisked from the airport to the British Embassy in a car with the blinds down. During his stay he visited General Nordenskjold in his HQ and was careful to enter and leave by the back door. It was known that the Germans photographed everyone visiting the Embassy and it was assumed that they would quickly identify the ex-Air Attache and realise that, as a friend of Nordenskjold's he had been sent over on a special mission. Thornton put it to the general that the British Expeditionary Force would not be able to overcome German resistance sufficiently quickly to prevent the murder of thousands of prominent Norwegians and the destruction of much of the infrastructure of Norway. The vast majority of the German army having been drawn off to repel the invasion, Norway's long frontier with Sweden would be wide open.

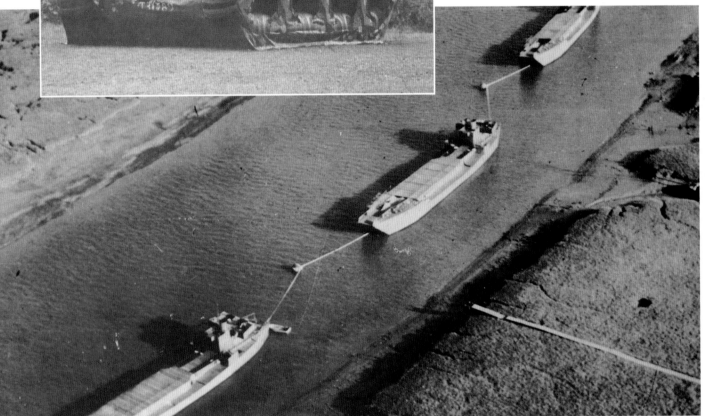

Left
Dummy Sherman Tank for
Operation Bodyguard.
Below
Dummy Tank Landing Craft
(LCT MkII) were used as decoys in south
east coast harbours when preparing for the
invasion of France. Of rigid construction,
designed by Messrs Cox & Co. of
Watford, this was 160 ft long, full size,
and launched in six hours.
Right
Sea vessels heavily camouflaged.
Below Right
A dummy 25 Pounder with Limber.

Thornton went on to propose that the Swedish Army should enter Norway, not as invaders, but as a police force to protect the rights of humanity. General Nordenskiold was deeply impressed and undertook to put his plan to the Swedish Government. Although he was known to be solidly pro-Allied, it was thought that there was a good chance that one of the Swedish ministers would inform the Germans of the plan. In fact, it was easier than that: the Swedish Chief of Police, who was pro-German, had 'bugged' the general's room. Every word of Thornton's and Nordenskjold's conversation was recorded and passed verbatim to the Germans. Within three hours Keitel had placed a report on Hitler's desk who immediately ordered a further 30,000 German troops into Norway. FORTITUDE NORTH was an outstanding success. A German force of over 200,000 men remained in Norway awaiting the invasion that never came.

FORTITUDE SOUTH was the deception plan to persuade the Germans that the Allies would invade the Pas de Calais. The main element of this plan, codenamed QUICK-SILVER, was the fictitious First United States Army Group (FUSAG) commanded by the very real General George Patton. FUSAG was revealed by radio traffic and through several double agents who provided their German handlers with detailed information on all the non-existent units assembling in Kent and East Anglia. Reality was added to the plan by including actual British, Canadian and US formations stationed in that area in the FUSAG order of battle. As these units in the days following D-Day were fed into the Normandy beachhead, they were replaced by a greater and greater proportion of fictitious units until by 26th august 1944, they had kept the threat to the Pas de Calais alive for as long as possible so that the Germans would be unable to reinforce Normandy from the Pas de Calais area. In the event, FUSAG fooled the German High Command longer than had been expected. It was the crucial deception.

In his weekly situation report on 25th June, three weeks after D-Day, von Runstedt stated that the enemy had still not committed the American Army Group assembled in south east England. He thought that they would be used for landings between the Somme and the Seine with the objective of encircling and capturing Le Havre. They would then join up with Montgomery's 21st Army Group to carry out a pincer attack on Paris. Thus thousands of men remained rooted in the east who might have turned the scales in Normandy. It is no exaggeration to say that, had it not been for FORTITUDE SOUTH, the battle in Normandy might well have turned out very differently.

ZEPPELIN was the codename given to cover the deception effort in south-eastern Europe. Its aim was to prevent the transfer of enemy troops from the eastern Mediterranean to northern France, in time to oppose the Allied landings in Normandy. This was done by concocting a threat against the Bulgarian and Romanian coasts by the Russians, a British attack through Greece, and an Anglo-American attack on Trieste, all culminating in a campaign in Austria and south Germany, leading to a large scale invasion of central Europe.

ZEPPELIN was also remarkably successful. During the period before OVERLOAD, not one German division moved from the Mediterranean to Northern Europe, and none arrived in time to influence the battle during the weeks after D-Day.

The main object of VENDETTA was to keep the maximum number of German troops in the south of France away from the Normandy beaches. This was to be done by staging a threat to that area; however, it was important that the threat should not be overdone as this could result in the Germans moving additional troops to the area which would then be manning the defences when in due course General 'Jumbo' Wilson launched Operation ANVIL, the genuine Allied invasion of southern France. Largely as a result of VENDETTA, Hitler left the German Army of the Riviera where it was.

The final component of BODYGUARD was IRONSIDE. This was designed to keep the 21st German Army in the Bordeaux area for at least the first three critical weeks after D-Day, by the threat of an invasion on the Biscay Coast. There is little evidence that IRONSIDE affected German strategic planning. Hitler was far more concerned with what he regarded as the four principal invasion threats to his 'Fortress Europe', namely through Norway, the Peloponnese, the French Riviera and the Pas de Calais.

When the Allies invaded on 6th June, some degree of tactical surprise was achieved, though this can mostly be put down to the appalling weather. With the exception of the German 352nd Infantry Division which happened to be on an anti-invasion exercise on the high ground behind Omaha Beach on D-Day, other units in Rommel's 7th Army were standing down and permitted to take local leave due to the storms in the Channel. Rommel was on his way to see his wife, and then go on to argue with Hitler at Berchtesgarten over the control of the Panzer reserves. But it is, of course, not the initial lodgement that is the most difficult part of a seaborne invasion - it is rather the ability to maintain and expand the initial foothold that is the real problem. The process of building up the bridgehead with follow-on forces and logistic resupply, making a breakout possible, requires both time and a degree of insulation from outside interference. The power and effectiveness of the German Panzer reserves was the main threat to the Normandy bridgehead. By persuading Hitler to keep the reserves and reinforcements, notably the 15th Army, out of Normandy until it was too late, and to disperse his forces all over Europe, BODYGUARD contributed massively to the successful Allied invasion of Europe.

What a difference 50 years makes,
it was worth it.

AIG Europe is proud to be the provider of Personal Accident Insurance to the British Armed Forces, including the recent action in the Gulf War, with PAX.

BY AIR TO BATTLE
THE BRITISH 6TH AIRBORNE DIVISION

*'Gentlemen, in spite of your excellent training and orders, do not be
daunted if chaos reigns, it undoubtedly will.'*

Brigadier S J L Hill DSO, MC
Commander 3rd Parachute Brigade

When General Sir Bernard Montgomery took over the command of 21st Army Group, one of his first decisions was to increase the width of the bridgehead to 50 miles. He allocated the task of shielding his flanks during the seaborne landings, and during the early part of the build-up to three airborne divisions. The British 6th Airborne Division was tasked with protecting the eastern flank and dominating the whole area east of Caen.

On his right flank, the United States 82nd and 101st Airborne Divisions were to land in the Cotentin peninsula, south of Cherbourg. Their tasks included seizing the causeways providing exits from Utah Beach, inland across the flooded land, and crossings over the River Merderet and its marshes.

On his left flank, Montgomery was concerned about the threat from German armour; in particular, that 21st Panzer Division and 12th SS (Hitler Jugend) Panzer Division, might counterattack through to the beachhead and roll up his assault division. He selected the River Orne and the Caen Canal as antiarmour obstacles on the eastern flank. About eight to ten miles to the east of the Orne, the River Dives flows north to the sea. Lying diagonally between the two river valleys, is a ridge of wooded country, with a thick forest, the Bois de Bavent, at its southern end. The commander of 6th Airborne, Major General Richard Gale, was given three primary tasks. The bridges over the River Orne and Caen canal at Benouville were to be seized intact. A battery of guns in concrete casemates at Merville was to be silenced half an hour before first light, at the latest, to prevent them firing on Sword Beach. To impose the maximum delay on enemy armour approaching from the east, the Division was to blow the road bridges over the River at Troarn, Bures Robehomme and Varaville, and the road and rail bridges at Bures. As soon as possible, but without prejudice to the success of the primary tasks, the Division was to deny to the enemy the area between the Dives and the Orne, and from Caen to the sea. It was to be reinforced by 1st Special Service Brigade (Commandos), under Brigadier the Lord Lovat, who having landed on Sword Beach, would march to join them later. Later on D-Day, the British 3rd Infantry Division would

Opposite
*A stick of parachute soldiers
emplaning in a Stirling.*

arrive to take over the defence of the area from Benouville to
the west, including the two bridges.

Major General Gale, inspired his division to train and fight
with a will. *"Go to it,"* ' he said, *'let that be your motto in all you do.'*
They did. His Division was organised as follows:

HQ 6th AIRBORNE DIVISION
Major General RN Gale

3rd PARACHUTE BRIGADE
Brigadier S J L Hill
8th & 9th PARACHUTE BATTALIONS
1st CANADIAN PARACHUTE BATTALION

5th PARACHUTE BRIGADE
Brigadier J H N Poett
7th, 12th & 13th PARACHUTE BATTALIONS

6th AIRLANDING BRIGADE
Brigadier the Hon H K M Kindersley
12th BATTALION THE DEVONSHIRE REGIMENT
2nd BATTALION THE OXFORDSHIRE
& BUCKINGHAMSHIRE LIGHT INFANTRY
1st BATTALION THE ROYAL ULSTER RIFLES

DIVISIONAL TROOPS
22nd INDEPENDENT PARACHUTE COMPANY
(PATHFINDERS)
6th AIRBORNE ARMOURED RECONNAISSANCE
REGIMENT RAC

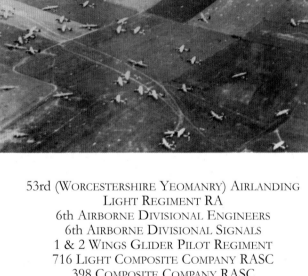

53rd (WORCESTERSHIRE YEOMANRY) AIRLANDING
LIGHT REGIMENT RA
6th AIRBORNE DIVISIONAL ENGINEERS
6th AIRBORNE DIVISIONAL SIGNALS
1 & 2 WINGS GLIDER PILOT REGIMENT
716 LIGHT COMPOSITE COMPANY RASC
398 COMPOSITE COMPANY RASC
224 & 225 PARACHUTE FIELD AMBULANCE
195 AIRLANDING FIELD AMBULANCE
6 AIRBORNE DIVISION WORKSHOPS REME

Except for the Canadians, all parachute battalions in 6th
Airborne Division had been formed from infantry battalions,
who had been asked to volunteer as a complete unit. The
majority did. After further selection, which about 130 all
ranks passed, they were brought up to full strength with additional volunteers. The core of the original battalion, with its

GIBBS MEW

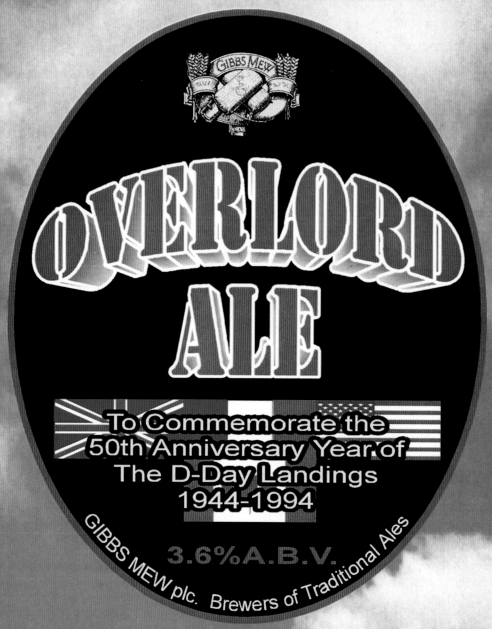

OVERLORD ALE

To Commemorate the
50th Anniversary Year of
The D-Day Landings
1944-1994

3.6% A.B.V.

GIBBS MEW plc. Brewers of Traditional Ales

**OVERLORD BREWED AT THE ANCHOR BREWERY
TO COMMEMORATE THE ALLIED LANDING IN 1944**

**FOR EVERY PINT SOLD UNTIL AUGUST 31ST 1994 A DONATION
WILL BE MADE TO S.S.A.F.A. AND THE ROYAL BRITISH LEGION.**

GIBBS MEW PLC, ANCHOR HOUSE, NETHERHAMPTON ROAD, SALISBURY,
WILTSHIRE SP2 8RA
TELEPHONE: SALISBURY (0722) 411911

THE ARMY IS GETTING SMALLER. WHY DO WE NEED MORE RECRUITS?

You've no doubt heard that the British Armed Forces are being streamlined as a result of the end of the Cold War.

We've pulled large numbers of troops out of Germany and reduced the level of our commitment in many other foreign locations.

Britain is not alone in taking this action.

The decreased threat of global warfare, coupled with a new willingness to negotiate arms controls, has brought about significant changes in all the world's major military forces.

So why, as the "peace dividend" begins to take effect, is the British Army looking to recruit more officers and soldiers? Events in the Gulf

and the on-going conflicts in Bosnia demonstrate that the world is still far from peaceful.

So the need for a modern, professional Army remains just as great as ever.

Indeed, with Britain's leading role in humanitarian relief and other UN operations, not to mention its membership of the newly formed NATO Rapid Reaction Corps, the Army has arguably an even greater role to play in world affairs.

However, like any large organisation, the Army has a high turnover of personnel.

Every year a great many people retire,

or simply leave to pursue alternative careers. But, unlike most organisations, we rely more heavily on the under 25s.

Which is why, despite the cut backs, we still need to recruit around 12,000 young men and women for officer and soldier positions this year.

This new influx will guarantee that the proud record of the British Army goes marching on. This influx will also ensure that, though reduced in size, our ability to respond to any situation won't be diminished. Quite the reverse, in fact. And whilst these newcomers use their talents to benefit us, we will do everything we can to benefit them.

Nowadays training is designed to build character as well as muscles.

We teach recruits how to cope under pressure, how to take charge of situations and how to use their new-found

skills to their best advantage.

They use some of the world's most sophisticated equipment and weapons technology.

If they have sporting aspirations, we hone them. We can even equip soldiers with one or more of up to 135 civilian trades. Plus

NVQs and transferable skills that will stand them in good stead should they want to leave the Army in the future.

What's more, because the British Army is still actively involved in many countries, it's still a good

way to see a bit of the world. And even, as in Bosnia, help with some of its problems.

So, while it is true to say the Army is getting smaller, the rewards of being in it are a good deal greater.

For more information about the Army, its opportunities and what they can mean for you, without obligation to join, visit your local Army Careers Office or call us on 0345 300 111.

ARMY
MORE OF A JOB.
MORE OF A LIFE.

Two of the three gliders by the Caen Canal Bridge (Pegasus Bridge), at Benouville.

regimental spirit, provided a foundation on which to build five magnificent battalions; as their performance in Normandy and later in the war would demonstrate. The infantry for the glider-borne role was also found by converting standard infantry battalions. Again, this proved very successful, as they brought with them their esprit de corps and cohesion. Although to the uninitiated their method of riding to battle lacked the glamour of parachuting, in reality it was sometimes more dangerous, and usually unpleasant. The motion of a glider under tow was such that many soldiers were sick within a few minutes, and sometimes the floor of the glider would be awash with vomit.

Pilots for gliders were found from volunteers from the Army. After landing, the pilots might not be extracted from the battle area for days or weeks. Rather than idly sitting about, they could play a useful part, and were trained not only to fly, but also to fight on the ground. Two types of glider were used on operations by the British in June 1944. The most numerous were the Horsas; each could carry 29 soldiers, or a jeep and trailer. The second type, the Hamilcar, the largest aircraft made of wood in the Second World War, weighed 14 tons fully-loaded, and could carry a light tank or a 17 pounder anti-tank gun. Gliders were towed by bombers or

transport aircraft from the launching airfield, and were released by the tug aircraft to glide down to the landing zone (LZ). It was not so easy as it sounds. A senior airman commented, *'It is equivalent to force-landing the largest size aircraft without engine aid ..... there is no higher test of pilot skill.'*

The aircraft providing tugs for the gliders and for parachuting were provided by 38 and 46 Group Royal Air Force. Number 38 Group was equipped with converted bombers, Albemarles, Halifaxes and Stirlings. Troops jumped from these through a hole cut in the floor for the purpose. Number 46 Group was equipped with the American C-47 Dakota, the great transport work-horse of the Second World War and for years afterwards. It was popular with parachute soldiers, not least because as one put it, *'one could leave like a gentleman through a door'.*

General Gale's plan was for Major John Howard's D Company of 2nd Battalion the Oxfordshire & Buckinghamshire Light Infantry (the old 52nd Light Infantry) to land by glider right by the Orne and Caen Canal bridges at 20 minutes after midnight on 6th June and seize them by *coup de main.* At the same time, 22nd Independent Parachute Company, the Division's pathfinders, were to parachute on to

bridges to the Canadians. The bulk of Kindersley's Airlanding Brigade would arrive by glider on the evening of D-Day. He was ordered to expand the bridgehead to the south to include Longueval, St Honorine la Chardonerette and Escoville.

Just before 23:00 hours on 5th June, six Halifaxes towing the six Horsa gliders carrying Major John Howard's company, took off from Tarrant Rushton in Dorset. Seven minutes later they were followed by Albemarles from Harwell, carrying the pathfinders of 22nd Independent Parachute Company, Brigadier Poett's tactical headquarters, and a special advance party, commanded by Major Allen Parry, for the 9th Parachute Battalion's attack on the Merville Battery. To maintain surprise, the take-off timings were calculated so that the pathfinders landed at the same time as Howard's *coup de main* force. The leading Albemarle was piloted by Squadron Leader Merrick, with Air Vice Marshall Leslie Hollingshurst, the Air Officer Commanding 38 Group, as his co-pilot.

The tug aircraft released their tows 5,000 feet over Caen. The pilots put the noses of their gliders sharply down and descended rapidly to about 1,000 feet, before levelling out, and descending again, turning twice, to run in to the LZs by the two bridges. The leading glider of the three destined for the Caen canal bridge landed on the exact spot planned during the briefing in England, the other two 15 and 25 yards away, a remarkable feat of airmanship. The leading platoon smashed their way out of their glider and charged across the bridge behind their platoon commander Lieutenant Brotheridge. Halfway across he was hit in the neck, dying 30 minutes later. Soon the bridge was firmly in the hands of Howard's men. One of the three gliders destined for the River Orne bridge landed five miles away, having been ordered to make a blind release by the tug captain. The other two landed 300 and 700 yards away, and the bridge was found undefended. The operation was a brilliant success. With remarkably few casualties, Major John Howard's soldiers, the first British troops to land in occupied France on D-Day, had taken the two vital bridges. Now they must be held. Fifth Parachute Brigade were on their way.

By the time the Albemarles with the pathfinders reached the coast, the cloud cover had increased, and the wind was gusting between 10 to 30 mph. Two sticks of pathfinders should have been dropped on each DZ, but in the event only one stick was dropped accurately on each. All the radar and visual beacons for DZ V were lost or damaged. One aircraft carrying a team for DZ K dropped them on DZ N, where, not realising they were on the wrong DZ, they set up their beacons and lights giving out the signals for DZ K. As a result, a large number of Pearson's Battalion landed on DZ N, as did some of Hill's headquarters.

The first of 5th Parachute Brigade to arrive on DZ N was Brigadier Nigel Poett and his tactical headquarters. He had decided that he must drop at the same time as the pathfinders, 30 minutes ahead of his brigade, so that he could take control if the *coup de main* on the bridges failed. As he walked briskly towards the bridges, he had no means of knowing if the attack had succeeded, because he could not find the officer carrying his radio. He learned later he had been killed soon after landing. Brigadier Poett, with one other member of his headquarters, arrived at the Orne Bridge 30 minutes after landing, to learn the good news of the capture of both bridges intact.

three Dropping Zones (DZs), to set up beacons to guide in the aircraft dropping the two parachute brigades at 50 minutes past midnight. Poett's 5th Parachute Brigade would drop on DZ N, move with utmost speed to reinforce Howard's company; hold the lodgement astride the bridges; and clear LZs to allow 68 gliders to land north of Ranville, bringing in Divisional Headquarters and anti-tank guns to assist Poett in holding off the German armour. Gale's orders to Poett were, *'The whole of your area must be held. Infantry positions will be fought to the last round and your anti-tank guns to the muzzle'*. The tasks allotted to Brigadier Hill's 3rd Parachute Brigade were: silencing the guns of the Merville Battery; destroying the five bridges over the Dives; and, on completion of the first two, holding the ridge running north-west from the Bois de Bavent.

Lieutenant Colonel Alastair Pearson's 8th Parachute Battalion was to drop on DZ K. Pearson was to destroy the bridges at Troarn and Bures, and deny the Bois de Bavent to the enemy. Lieutenant Colonel Terence Otway's 9th Parachute Battalion and Lieutenant Colonel Bradbrook's 1st Canadian Parachute Battalion were to drop on DZV. The silencing of the Merville Battery was allocated to the 9th Battalion, and the blowing of the Varaville and Robehomme

DZ N was easier for the air crews to locate than the other two, because they could see the Orne and the Canal, and the fireworks round the bridge where Howard's men were fighting off the first counter-attacks. So on the whole the drop of 5th Parachute Brigade went well, although it was widely spread. In 23 minutes 123 aircraft dropped 2,026 men and 702 containers. Many sticks were blown by the strong westerly wind to the eastern side of the DZ, and overloaded men were slow getting out of the aircraft, so adding to the dispersion. Some were dropped in Ranville, still held by the Germans, and were killed, wounded or taken prisoner.

First of the main body to arrive at the bridges was Lieutenant Colonel Geoffrey Pine-Coffin's 7th Battalion. Poett sent them straight across to Benouville and Le Port. Lieutenant Colonel Johnny Johnston's 12th Battalion and Lieutenant Colonel Peter Luard's 13th Battalion had tasks east of the bridges. Lieutenant Jack Watson, commanding 3 Platoon of A Company, 13th Battalion remembers:

I landed at the north end of the DZ in an orchard. Everything was quiet and I thought I was miles away from Ranville, the battalion objective. But then I saw the distinctive tower of Ranville church to the south where it should have been. As I moved towards the RV, a wood north of the village, I heard loud and shrill, the sounds of hunting horns: the CO sounding 'L' for Lancashire [the 13th Battalion had originally been 2/4th South Lancashires], and the company calls 'A' for A Company and so on. The DZ was a real bugger's muddle with people from all three battalions from our brigade, and some of the 8th who had been dropped on the wrong DZ. But our hunting horns cut through clearly, I got to the RV, the company was about 40 strong. About half an hour later we were up to 60 [less than two-thirds strength]. But I was missing a section and my platoon sergeant. My company commander decided to wait no longer and we set off to clear the DZ of poles for the first wave of gliders. The remainder of the Battalion moved off and after a sharp fight, captured Ranville, the first village in France to be liberated.

Jack Watson's platoon sergeant, Arthur Lawley:

When the green light came on, number one jumped followed by the remainder up to number ten, a bren gunner carrying a very heavy load. He fell across the exit, preventing anyone else from jumping. The only one who could help him to his feet was the RAF despatcher. This took time, during which the plane circled the DZ three times before I could jump. As soon as I was airborne, I realised my rifle, kit bag and shovel have broken away from me. I landed in a cornfield. I lay quite still, listening: in the distance I could hear the noise of battle and guessed it must be the DZ, I had gone some distance, when I saw three bent figures. I got up close, challenged, and to my relief they were our chaps. Guided by the Battalion call blown by Colonel Luard on a hunting horn, we were soon at the RV.

The sound of battle Arthur Lawley heard was from the Caen Canal bridge, he, and others like him, by marching towards the sound of the guns like the good soldiers they were, crossed the DZ and found their RVs.

Hill's 3rd Parachute Brigade had a very scattered drop. Major Allen Parry waiting by the 9th Battalion RV, after hearing the aircraft carrying his battalion passing overhead, expected soldiers to come streaming off the DZ. Instead, they trickled in. Lieutenant Colonel Otway's plan for silencing the formidable Merville Battery involved a quantity of special equipment and a variety of parties arriving on time. Three gliders

were to crash-land on the Battery, relying on the concrete constructions to tear off the wings, thus arresting the progress of the fuselages. Out of these would spring 60 men of A Company and eight Royal Engineers. Simultaneously the main body of the Battalion, having marched from their DZ 2,200 yards away, would blow three gaps in the defences and charge in, joining the glider party in killing the defenders. The guns would be destroyed by the Engineers using explosive charges. Before the Battalion left for the Battery, five more gliders were to land on the DZ carrying jeeps, and anti-tank guns to blast the armoured doors of each casemate, scaling ladders with which to cross the anti-tank ditch on the northeast side; and a quantity of other men and equipment, including mortars to fire illuminating bombs to light the way in for the crash-landing gliders, mine detectors to clear lanes through a minefield round all but one side of the objective and white tape to mark the cleared paths, more engineers and explosive, Bangalore Torpedoes to blast gaps in the barbed wire, and Vickers medium machine guns. Before the show started, 13 Lancasters and 86 Halifaxes were to drop 1,000-pound bombs on the battery.

The crews of the squadron dropping the 9th Battalion made every effort to cope with the total lack of beacons on DZ V. But as the DZ was only one minute's flying time from the coast, there was little time for the pilots to orientate themselves before the run-in and the drop. All but the lead aircraft were buffeted by the slipstreams of the others. Before crossing the coast the soldiers were standing hooked up, many were thrown to the floor as the Dakotas bucked and lurched. By the time the heavily-laden parachute soldiers had regained their feet, the aircraft had overshot the DZ. Some pilots in aircraft that had not dropped all their stick came round for another try, banking steeply in the turn and making it difficult for soldiers to scramble up or keep their balance. After another tight turn the aircraft joined the stream, a hair-raising performance in the blackness. The problem of locating the DZ, often after several passes, combined with the westerly wind, resulted in the drop of the 9th Battalion being scattered over 50 square miles. Nearly two hours after the drop, only 150 all ranks out of a strength of 700 had reported to the RV. Other than a few lengths of Bangalore Torpedo and one machine gun, none of the special equipment, or specialists arrived. The commanding officer remembers that for about five minutes his mind went blank as the enormity of the situation dawned on him. Then with no thought other than his determination to carry out his task, he gave the order to implement the plan with his meagre resources. As a final blow, none of the crash-landing gliders landed on the battery. One landed near Odiham, having broken its tow rope. One landed on the other side of the River Dives, and the third about 1,000 yards south-east of the battery where the occupants under the command of Lieutenant Hugh Pond did sterling work holding off Germans approaching from the direction of Gonneville.

Lieutenant Hugh Pond:

One of my chaps had a flame-thrower. Over the Battery we were hit by light anti-aircraft fire. One round hit the flame-thrower. The glider and the unfortunate chap were on fire for the last few seconds of the approach. As we swooped in, we saw the battery. We lifted over a wire fence, which we thought was outside the battery, and crash-landed in an orchard some distance away. As we all rushed out, except the poor chap

Synchronising watches before take-off, evening of 5 June 1944, l to r: Lieutenants Robert de Latour, Donald Wells, John Vischer and Captain Robert Midwood of 22nd Independent Parachute Company, before emplaning in Albermarles at RAF Harwell.

on fire, we heard shooting, which we realised was the battalion in the battery.

As the glider vanished, Otway ordered gaps blown in the wire with the few remaining Bangalore Torpedoes, and four assault parties dashed in, led by Major Allen Parry, Lieutenant Alan Jefferson, CSM Barney Ross and Colour Sergeant Harold Long. Each party headed for one of the four casemates, under fire and hindered by bomb craters, uncut wire and mines. Jefferson and Parry were wounded. On reaching the casemates, they found not the 150 mm guns they had been led to expect, but 100 mm Czech howitzers.

Without means to destroy the guns, the gallant assault by this sorely depleted battalion killed, captured or drove off the gun crews, thereby preventing them from firing the guns for a few vital hours. In the process they lost 65 killed, wounded or missing. As they withdrew to a preselected RV, a few late-arrivals came in, bringing the Battalion strength to about 80. They set off for their objective, the village of Le Plein.

The attack on the Merville Battery epitomises the spirit that imbued all the soldiers of 6th Airborne Division. Almost everything that could go wrong did so. But well trained, well briefed, determined soldiers, taking advantage of the cover of darkness, were not deterred by chaos, to which their adversary was equally subjected, but using surprise, turned it to their advantage, doing all that was humanly possible to fulfil their allotted tasks.

Lieutenant Colonel Alastair Pearson arrived at his Battalion RV to find 30 men there. Two and a half hours after the drop, he had only 156 out of his battalion of over 600. But personal initiative and leadership at all levels ended in the battalion achieving all its tasks. The Canadians, despite losses due to their scattered drop also fulfilled their missions.

Brigadier James Hill, whose words, quoted at the beginning, had proved so prophetic, arrived at his headquarters in the afternoon of D-Day. Like many of his brigade he was dropped in the flooded valley of the River Dives. Here many drowned, weighed down by their equipment, or falling exhausted into deep ditches that criss-crossed the area, invisible under waist-deep flood water. After four hours wading, having collected together 42 others, Brigadier Hill's party was bombed by friendly aircraft, killing or wounding all but eight of the party, including the Brigadier. Despite this, he pressed on, visiting the 9th Battalion en route, eventually reaching Divisional Headquarters. Here, having refused to be evacuated, he was operated on by the senior doctor in the division, before being driven to his headquarters, where he found Lieutenant Colonel Pearson, who had been shot through the hand on the DZ that morning, temporarily in command of the brigade.

Throughout D-Day the German high command was in confusion. By 05:30 hours Brigadier General Feuchtinger, commanding 21st Panzer Division, had sufficient intelligence to build up a clear picture of 6th Airborne Divisions disposi-

tions in Ranville and on the Bois de Bavent ridge. His request to Army Group B for permission to attack was refused. He asked again at about 07:30 hours and was allowed to send two Panzer grenadier battalions to attack Ranville. Finally, General Speidel at Army Group B released the whole of 21st Panzer division. This news took two hours to reach Feuchtinger, whose troops were approaching their start lines to attack Ranville, Le Bas de Ranville and Herouvillette; some 120 tanks and 3,000 infantry pitted against three weak parachute battalions, a glider infantry company, some gunners and sappers, six 6-pounder and three 17-pounder anti-tank guns. At that juncture, Feuchtinger's orders were changed, to switch his main effort to the west of the Orne towards the beaches where the sea-borne assault was in full swing. Chaos ensued, and although a few tanks penetrated to the coast, they withdrew when 6th Airlanding Brigade arrived, thinking they were landing among the rear elements of the Division round Caen. Order and counter-order prevented the whole 21st Panzer Division from carrying out a coordinated attack against Ranville and Herouvillette, although several armoured attacks accompanied by infantry were mounted at up to regimental strength. These were mainly repulsed by 7th and 12th Parachute Battalions. When Lovat, leading his commandos and preceded by his piper, arrived at the Caen Canal Bridge, it was an emotional moment, but with little opportunity to savour it. General Gale held back one of Lovat's commandos in case the defence of the bridges needed buttressing. In the event, it was not needed.

As evening approached, the weary defenders of the bridges were treated to the marvellous sight of 248 gliders carrying 6th Airlanding Brigade to the LZs just to their north. Major Nigel Taylor, commanding A Company, of the 7th Battalion, wounded after fighting all day in Benouville saw them arrive:

'Soon after, all these fit, fresh chaps came pouring over the bridges. I thought, we've done it'.

They had, but there was yet more to do in the ensuing battle of Normandy. The events of D-Day had only been a beginning, there was much bitter fighting, particularly in the six days following the dramatic events of 6th June. During this time, the division well below strength because of battle casualties and sticks dropped wide, held their ground against increasingly well coordinated counter-attacks. For days, some of the parachute battalions were down to little over the equivalent of a company in strength. As a measure of the intensity of the battle, on 7th June alone, Major Howard's D Company, 52nd Light Infantry, which had captured the bridges with so few casualties only 36 hours before, suffered 50% casualties fighting at Escoville. The Division, with 1st and 4th Special Service Brigades under command, was to remain in the bridgehead until mid-August, when they advanced to the Seine on the left of the Canadian Army.

The fighting in Normandy cost 6th Airborne Division a total of 4,457 killed, wounded and missing.

THE RAF ROLE IN THE AIRBORNE OPERATION

The airborne invasion of Normandy by Allied parachute troops started when D-Day was only 20 minutes old and had been completed more than two hours before the first landing craft had reached the beaches.

The precedent for Allied airborne assaults had been far from encouraging. Early airborne operations had involved

Briefing glider pilots and tug crews before D-Day.

small scale forces but OPERATION HUSKY, the first major Allied airborne assault which opened the invasion of Sicily in July 1943, showed the dangers inherent in this kind of assault. This operation was undertaken at night and resulted in serious aircraft losses (including many from friendly fire) and wildly-inaccurate drops highlighting the need for improved navigational techniques and a higher degree of co-ordination between all assault force components.

The British airborne assault plan for D-Day was split into three complementary phases: OPERATION TONGA called for the dropping of two parachute brigade groups of the British 6th Airborne Division between the rivers Orne and Dives; OPERATION MALLARD was the delivery by glider of the remainder of the 6th Division just before dusk; and OPERATION ROB ROY was the re-supply effort. At the same time the American 82nd and 101st Airborne divisions were to be dropped by the USAAF's IX Troop Carrier Command near St Mere-Eglise some 50 miles to the west of the British positions.

The RAF organisations tasked with the airborne operations were Nos. 38 and 46 Groups based at airfields in central southern England. No.46 Group consisted of five squadrons of the ubiquitous Dakota which had already proved itself as an outstanding transport aircraft. The Dakota squadrons were based at Broadwell (Nos. 512 and 575 Squadrons), Down Ampney (48 and 271), and Blakehill Farm (233). No.38 Group was equipped with three different types of aircraft, all converted bombers and none ideal for air transport operations. The twin-engined Albemarle, which had been found to be unsuitable as a bomber, equipped four squadrons at Brize Norton (296 and 297) and Harwell (295 and 570) while the four-engined Stirling equipped a further four squadrons at Fairford (190 and 620) and Keevil (196 and 299). Finally, two squadrons of Halifaxes were based at Tarrant Rushton (298 and 644) and were the only aircraft powerful enough to tow the huge Hamilcar glider with any degree of safety.

For the Overlord operation the RAF used two types of assault glider. The basic troop-carrying glider was the Airspeed Horsa which could carry up to 31 including the two pilots who were expected to fight with the airborne troops after landing. The Horsa handled well even when fully loaded and a total of 3,655 were made during the war. The General Aircraft Hamilcar was a much larger glider capable of carrying light tanks, field guns or other heavy equipment up to a maximum load of 19,000 lbs. A total of 412 Hamilcars were built and more than a hundred were lost during the war.

OPERATION TONGA was intended as a glider borne landing but when the Germans set up extensive obstacles in likely landing areas in April it was decided to use parachute troops for the initial assault instead. Dropped from six Albermarles of Nos. 295 and 570 Squadrons at 00:20 hours on 6th June the first airborne forces to touch French soil were the pathfinders of 22nd Independent Parachute Company who were to locate and mark the dropping zones (DZs) for the main force. Almost simultaneously six Halifaxes from Nos. 298 and 644 Squadrons released their Horsa gliders to deposit their troops close to two vital bridges between Benouville and Ranville. The accurate flying of tug and glider pilots enabled the swift success of this particular operation. About 30 minutes later the main force arrived to be dropped

at DZs K, N and V from 250 aircraft. The main force was followed nearly three hours later by the Divisional HQ troops carried in 68 Horsas and four Hamilcar gliders which landed successfully and DZ N.

The initial parachute drop did not go entirely according to plan but the Germans were completely taken by surprise. The Horsa and Hamilcar pilots of the Glider Pilot Regiment took up arms as soon as they had landed and unloaded their charges and 34 died fighting alongside the paratroopers.

Operation Tonga had met with mixed success. Although many of the drops were scattered the troops eventually achieved all their objectives. Aircraft attrition was lighter than expected, out the 264 transport aircraft which took off on the operation only seven were lost.. The gliders had fared less well, 22 out of 98 missing and only 57 landing on or near to the DZs, but it must be said that the gliders had the most dif-

ficult task and the glider pilots acquitted themselves brilliantly under the circumstances. A total of 5,123 troops were carried on Operation Tonga of whom 4,803 were landed.

The transport crews were ready for take off again by 17:00 hrs on the evening of D-Day for the next major airborne operation. MALLARD, which would take the remainder of 6th Airborne Division to Normandy. This operation benefitted from the efforts of the troops landed during Tonga and was a great success which was especially encouraging as it was the RAF's first large scale daylight glider operation. A total of 256 aircraft/glider combinations took off, 146 destined for DZ N and 110 for DZ W a mile north of Pegasus Bridge. All No. 38 and 46 Group squadrons took part with the exception of No. 233 Squadron which was preparing for the first re-supply mission. The gliders, which included 30 Hamilcars loaded with vehicles and heavy weapons, landed just before dusk at 21:00 hrs to enable the transports to return to England under the cover of darkness. Only two aircraft were lost during operation Mallard and 95 per cent of the gliders landed their troops successfully to link up with and reinforce their comrades who had been fighting since the early hours of the morning.

Dropping Zone N just outside Ranville was selected as the most suitable destination for the re-supply effort and the first of the OPERATION ROB ROY missions was flown by 50 Dakotas on the evening of 6 June. Unfortunately, this formation met the problem which had ruined the airborne landings during OPERATION HUSKY, the aircraft overflew Royal Navy ships which opened fire on them, bringing one down and splitting the formation. The drop was consequently scattered and five of the Dakotas were lost to German flak. Stirlings flew two more re-supply missions on 8 June although the second mission was affected by bad weather which forced half the formation to return without dropping. Two more successful drops on 10 June brought OPERATION ROB ROY to a conclusion although regular re-supply missions continued to be flown under the codename OPERATION TOWNHALL throughout the summer.

Left
Tugs and gliders on an airfield.
Below
Tugs and gliders approaching the French coast on the evening of D-Day.

NAVAL
OPERATIONS

The invasion of Normandy was possible only because, by the summer of 1944, the Allies largely commanded the air and sea approaches to the invasion area. But although the German navy and air force had by this time in effect been defeated, the Allied victory was by no means complete. For the invasion to succeed, a number of threats at sea would have to be contained at least, both before and during the landing operation.

The first of these was the menace of the German U-boats. Intelligence had revealed that the Germans had ear-marked the 36 U-boats of the Landwirte Group for anti-invasion duties.

Moreover, some of these submarines were equipped with 'schnorkels' which meant they could stay underwater for much longer, running on diesels rather than electric motors.

They were also known to have torpedoes especially suited for shallow waters and a number of sophisticated deception devices.

Since the water conditions were likely to be very difficult for anti-submarine operations, U-boats, on the face of it, could have wreaked havoc amongst the invasion forces, just as they had in the Dardanelles in 1915.

HMS Beagle with three LST's in the background.

46

But although the Allies took this threat seriously and allocated over 200 ships for anti-submarine duties, they were confident of their ability to contain this threat.

Coastal Command aircraft now operated almost continuous air patrols which made it very hazardous for U-boats to surface anywhere in the area; in fact all non-Schorkel U-boats were ordered back to port on 12th June because of this. But even the schnorkel boats proved less useful than the Germans had hoped; their progress underwater was slow and prolonged submergence had distressing effects on the crew. In the first two days of the operation, Coastal Command sank or damaged a quarter of the Landwirte U-boats, and Allied ships successfully kept the survivors at arms length.

Only on 28th June, three weeks after D-Day, did the U-boats have their first success against invasion shipping. It might have been a different story if the Germans had then been able to operate their new Type XXI and XXIII U-boats of 1945, but as it was the submarine threat was easily mastered.

It was much the same story as regards the remnants of the German surface navy. The Germans had a force of powerful Narvik and Elbing class destroyers in the area and these had to be watched constantly. Two days after the landing, at dusk on June 8th, they left Brest for a foray against the invasion shipping. But they were quickly intercepted by the 10th Destroyer Flotilla. In the early hours of 9th June, one German destroyer was sunk, another wrecked ashore and the survivors, badly mauled, fled back to Brest; they took no further part in the Normandy campaign.

The German E-boat squadrons operating out of Brest and Le Havre were a different matter, however. These fast deadly torpedo craft had provided a graphic warning of what they could accomplish on 28th April 1944 when a squadron of them had pounced on an American amphibious force exercising off Portland Bill. In a few minutes, they had sunk two LSTs and damaged another, killing over 600 men. The E-Boat was plainly a serious threat.

For this reason, the Allies deployed 138 Motor Torpedo Boats (MTB) into the area. The invasion shipping off the assault area was arranged into a large rectangle with a protective hedge of minesweepers around the defensive perimeter. Outside this perimeter, and indeed back to the British coast, squadrons of MTBs patrolled. A control ship with room for large modern radar controlled their movements, and scores of destroyers acted as a long-stop to deal with any E-boats that got through the British MYB screen.

The result was a fast murderous battle that took place most nights after the invasion began. Each engagement was over in seconds if not minutes, fought at close range with bofors and heavy machine guns. Tracer fire and the occasional burning craft lit up the darkness.

Whenever, the E-Boats broke through, they were checked

by destroyers firing AA shells set to explode 20 feet above and in front of their speeding targets, drenching them with shrapnel. Their bases at Le Havre and Cherbourg were subjected to devastating attacks by RAF Mosquito bombers. The E-boats losses were severe with 16 sunk and 14 badly damaged in the ten days after D-Day. The E-boats scored a few successes amongst the invasion shipping but their overall strategic effect was negligible.

Mines were probably the most serious maritime threat of all to the allied invasion fleet. The Germans were known to have laid a series of offensive minefields off the English coast, and defensive ones off the French coast. There was also a large moored minefield some seven to ten miles off the French coast. Through these dense minefields, the shipping of five invasion fleets had to pass and repass. Moreover, once the Allies had revealed where the main invasion had taken place, the Germans would surely mount a major mining campaign using aircraft and surface ships. The consequent losses to the dense mass of shipping supporting the invasion could have been catastrophic.

To combat this threat, the Allies deployed over 250 sweepers and support craft in the biggest mine-sweeping operation of the war. The task of this force was to cut two channels through the mines from the assembly point on the English coast to the disembarkation Zone on the French coast, for each of the five invasion forces. The shipping routes all converged at the approaches to the French coastline in a congested sea area that the Allies called 'the spout'. The likelihood of confusion and disaster was particularly acute in this area.

Once the invasion force had arrived, the channels would need to be enlarged to accommodate the build-up of shipping off the coast. Finally, the minesweepers would have to clear areas for warships engaged in bombardment.

The minesweeping forces set to work, clearing the mines and laying lighted Dan buoys every mile or so on both sides of the cleared channel. With the complex cross-tides of the Channel and the ever present possibility of ambush by German E-boats, this was a far from easy task. Nevertheless it was successfully accomplished.

Although there were a few mistakes, with elements of some invasion fleets going down the wrong cleared channels, the minesweepers and Dan buoy layers had completed their complex task so well that of the huge armada crossing to France only one LST and one destroyer escort , HMS Wrestler ,were struck by mines.

The biggest challenge, however was yet to come. After the invasion site was established, the Germans began to send single aircraft into the area, up to 50 a night, dropping parachute mines. This added to the huge numbers already there, many of the new mines appearing to land in areas already regarded as cleared. So dense were they in fact, that on one occasion a minesweeper switched on its electrical impulse gear and no less than 23 mines exploded in its immediate vicinity in a few seconds.

It soon became clear, however, that many of the mines were not of the magnetic or acoustic sort with which the minesweepers had by now become familiar. Minings became more rather than less common as the invasion operation went on. Whereas three ships were sunk and another 12 mined in the first ten days after 6th June, there was a sharp rise in casualties later on. No less than five ships were sunk and another two badly damaged between 20th-24th June.

The reason was only fully revealed when a German aircraft dropped its mine in shallow water from which it could be recovered at low tide. A mine-disposal officer took it to pieces and discovered it to be a mine activated by pressure. The Allies called these "Oyster " mines but had no real way of dealing with them.

From then on large ships in shallow waters moved very slowly to reduce their pressure waves. Battleships engaged in bombardment work often had to be towed into their bombardment position. But these were no more than palliatives, and the mining threat was never wholly mastered. Instead the counter-effort was aimed at the aircraft which dropped the mines, and the airfields from which they operated. Thus was the mine threat contained.

All of this was such a vast undertaking that the minesweeping effort had to be initiated as early as possible. Indeed, the 14th Minesweeping Flotilla had moved into its positions off the Normandy Coast at eight o'clock on the evening before the invasion, the 5th June. From this minesweeping position they were in sight of the French coast, and indeed could make out several individual houses on the coast-line; but so important was their task, that the risk of detection just had to be accepted.

Nor, in fact were they the first Allied vessels on the invasion scene. This honour fell to two five-man midget submarines, X 30 and X 23, whose task was to mark the exact landfall for Juno and Sword beaches.

In the past, and despite accurate preliminary reconnaissance, amphibious forces had often found it difficult to go ashore precisely where it was intended that they should.

Indeed, none of the Torch landings of November 1942 were in the right place and some were as much as eight miles off station. In this case, the eastern beaches in the assault area were particularly difficult to mark. And so to help avoid any repetition of this kind of thing, the two midget submarines with special crews took up their station three miles off the French coast, just about the time it was decided to postpone the landings for a day.

As a result, they submerged and waited, their crews breathing the increasingly foul air of their tiny vessels. But, exactly on schedule, both craft came to the surface just before sunrise on the morning of the 6th June, checked their positions and showed green lights for the invasion forces to use in their final approach to the French coast. By the time they returned to England, the two little submarines had been at sea for 76 hours, 64 of them submerged.

Opposite
MTB's returning from patrol.

WHAT WAS THE CONTRIBUTION OF NAVAL AVIATION?

Sixteen naval air squadrons flying from shore bases took part in Operation Neptune, one Dutch, three American and twelve Royal Navy air squadrons. Two of the US Navy squadrons flew Liberator anti-submarine patrol aircraft, operating against submarines in transit through the Bay of Biscay; the third squadron was the only US Navy unit ever to operate Spitfires. The single Royal Netherlands Navy squadron was equipped with B-25 Mitchell Bombers and flew as part of the 2nd Tactical Air Force's medium bomber force against inland targets.

The Royal Navy's contribution was more mixed, in equipment as well as in the tasks. The Swordfish of 838 Squadron provided night anti-E-boat patrols off the coast of Brittany. In the central Channel, in the invasion area, the Swordfish of 819 and Avengers of 848 operated by night against the E-boats, while on the extreme eastern flank two more Avenger squadrons, 854 and 855, supported the Dover Command's E-boat patrols. After the assault phase, some of the squadrons were moved to meet the changing requirements, notably the arrival of U-boats in the waters used by resupply convoys and the introduction of midget submarines. The Avengers occasionally found themselves in a completely unexpected combat role and this resulted in two 'kills' against V.1 flying bombs.

Seven fighter squadron (five of them naval) had perhaps the most unusual task. Spotting for the guns of the Fleet, whether in action against ships or shore targets, had been one of the very first tasks for shipborne aircraft, but by 1943 it was clear that the 'traditional' multi-seat spotter aircraft was too vulnerable to modern AA defences. In the autumn of that year, certain single-seater fighter squadrons began to train for the job and in the spring of 1944, No. 3 Naval Fighter Wing was moved to RNAS Lee-on-Solent as the nucleus of the Air Spotting Pool, to spot for the NEPTUNE battleship and cruiser shore bombardment forces. Besides the Seafires of 885 and 886 Squadrons and the Spitfires of 808 and 897 Squadrons, the Pool included two RAF Spitfire Squadrons, Nos 26 and 63, whose pilots had also been trained in this role, and VCS7, a US Navy unit whose pilots already knew the role but who had to accustom themselves to the high-performance landplane Spitfires after the float biplanes which they had previously flown from ships' catapults.

Pairs of spotters from Lee-on Solent were active over all the beaches from dawn on D-Day, correcting the fall of shot on batteries, enemy movements and key bridges and junctions up to 15 miles inland, identifying fresh targets for the guns and, during the opening days, occasionally fending off German fighters, several of which were shot down. VCS7 was withdrawn after the fall of Cherbourg in late June, but not until the second week in July were the enemy pushed back out of battleship gun in the Caen sector. Fewer bombardment targets were available, but this released some sorties for a task - dawn patrols against midget submarines, several of which were sunk by the "anti-submarine fighters". When, in mid-July, the Air Spotting Pool was disbanded, its Seafires and Spitfires had flown 1,230 sorties in 33 'flyable' days, for the loss of two dozen aircraft to flak, fighters and the weather but very few of the RN, USN and RAF pilots were lost. It had also proved the value of the fighter-spotter.

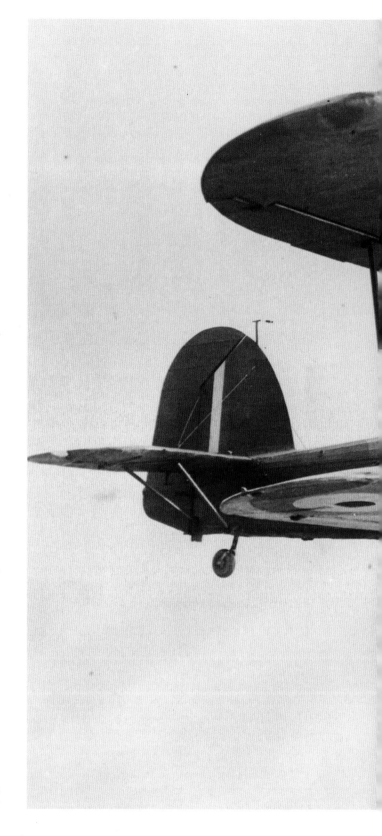

Few aeroplanes ever received such universal acclaim as the Swordfish. It earned the affection and respect of thousands of FAA pilots, who nick-named it the 'Stringbag'.

THE NAVAL BOMBARDMENT

Although a heavy air bombardment was planned to demolish the German defences it could not be relied upon alone to inflict sufficient damage, especially against the German shore batteries that covered the beaches. It was essential therefore to use warships to engage the German shore batteries during the assault and to drench the beach defences with fire to cover the landing forces. By the standards of land warfare naval guns were heavy weapons with enormous destructive power, especially those carried in the largest supporting warships.

Most impressive of the bombarding ships on D-Day were five battleships, two British and three American. All were old - there was too much work for modern battleships elsewhere - but all were formidable in the shore bombardment role with the capacity to fire shells of half a ton or more against the shore. The two Royal Navy ships were Warspite and Ramillies; neither could fire their full armament, the former having been damaged by a guided bomb while supporting landings in Italy and the latter having a reduced crew, but with six and four 15-inch guns respectively they were formidable opponents

HMS Rodney bombarding.

for the captured French 6.1-inch guns of the batteries at Villerville and Benerville.

The two British battleships were also covering the batteries around Le Havre, which included three 15-inch guns originally intended for the German battleship Bismarck. Covering the American beaches were the USS Nevada and Texas each with ten 14-inch guns and the Arkansas with twelve 12-inch weapons. Also carrying battleship-sized guns were the specialist shore bombardment monitors HMS Roberts and HMS Terror, each mounting a single twin 15-inch turret. One was placed on each flank of the landings, the latter having the 6.1-inch battery at Houlgate as primary target, the latter covering the 6.1-inch batteries at Cape Barfluer and La Pernelle.

The battleships and monitors were supplemented by cruisers, whose guns matched or exceeded in calibre those of the shore batteries. There were three American heavy cruisers each with nine 8-inch guns, three large British light

cruisers each with twelve 6-inch (one - HMS Belfast is preserved today in the Pool of London) three smaller modern British light cruisers armed with 6-inch guns and five armed with 5.25-inch weapons.

Older British cruisers, two armed with 7.5-inch and three with 6-inch guns found a new lease of life in the shore bombardment role. Another old 6-inch British cruiser was Polish-manned, while two Free French light cruisers Montcalm and Georges Leygues bombarded their native shore in support of the Americans on *Omaha* Beach. Also with the cruisers were two Dutch colonial gunboats, each armed with three 5.9-inch guns, one covering *Utah* Beach and the other *Gold*.

Between the heavy ships and the beaches moved almost 60 bombardment destroyers to smother the beach defences. The American landings were covered by 20 destroyers, mainly USN "Gleaves" and "Benson" class armed with four 5-inch guns apiece, supplemented by three British "Hunt" class escort destroyers each armed with four 4-inch weapons.

The eight American destroyers off *Omaha* Beach played a particularly crucial role in supporting the hard-pressed landing forces. Off the British and Canadian beaches were 39 destroyers, mainly of the standard British wartime fleet destroyer type armed with four 4.7-inch guns, but also supplemented by a few older ships armed with three to six 4.7-inch weapons, and 13 "Hunts".

Of these ships, two fleet destroyers were Canadian manned and two Norwegian, and of the "Hunts" one was Norwegian, two were Polish and one Free French.

In all over 100 ships were assigned bombardment roles including reserves, the largest of which were the 16-inch gun battleships HMS *Nelson* and HMS *Rodney* whose two-ton shells were not needed for the preliminary bombardment on D-Day itself. *Rodney* very briefly engaged the Le Havre batteries when they opened fire on the afternoon of 6th June, but only came properly into action on the following day. She was relieved off the beaches by HMS *Nelson* on 10th June.

Spotting for the guns was provided by specially trained pilots flying Spitfires. Some of these aircraft, that swooped low over the beaches to find their targets of opportunity once the shore batteries were neutralised, were flown by US Navy aircrew who had swapped their vulnerable seaplanes for the nimble British aircraft. Because of the massive ammunition expenditure of bombardment ships lighters loaded with shells were prepared at harbours in Britain to reload ships with the minimum of delay so they could be quickly back on station.

To provide close support for the troops on the beaches there were a number of heavily armed landing craft available. Larger tank landing craft (LCT) were converted to carry two 4.7-inch guns as Landing Craft Gun (Large), LCG(L). There were three of these at *Juno*, four at *Gold* and three at *Sword*. Other LCTs had been converted to carry light automatic guns in the anti-aircraft role as "Landing Craft Flak" (LCF) but they proved more useful against surface targets ashore and afloat. There were seven at *Gold*, six at *Juno* and five at *Sword*. At *Juno* were six smaller Landing Craft Support (Light) that carried a six-pounder Valentine tank turret on the forecastle. In addition were LCTs carrying armoured vehicles and self

propelled guns. At *Sword* and *Gold* were eight and ten vessels respectively each carrying Royal Marine-manned Centaur close support tanks with 95 mm howitzers; at *Sword* these were supplemented by a Landing Craft Gun (Medium) with two 17-pounder anti-tank guns in armoured turrets for demolishing bunkers. At *Juno* the above capabilities were replaced by tank landing craft carrying four self-propelled artillery regiments. At *Gold* and *Sword* there were also small "Hedgerow" assault landing craft (LCA) fitted with 24 60-pound mortars for cleaning a path through minefields.

Most spectacular of the close support bombardment vessels was the LCT (Rocket) packed with 792 5-inch rocket

54

projectiles that were designed to drench a landing area with fire just before touch down. There were eight of these at *Juno*, seven at *Gold* and five at *Sword*. Nine LCT (R) were also covering the *Omaha* landings. The close gunfire support group there also included seven LCF, five LCG(L), 16 LCT equipped with close support tanks and ten with self-propelled artillery. *Utah* was covered by four LCT(R), four LCG, four LCF and eight LCT equipped with close support tanks.

The performance of the bombarding ships was declared to be "magnificent" by Rear Admiral Alan G. Kirk commander of the Western Task Force (85) and Admiral Sir Bertram Ramsay concluded that their shooting had been "uniformly good". It had "helped in no small measure" to ensure the success of both the landing and the initial Allied advance off the beaches.

HMS Warspite bombarding the battery at Villerville.

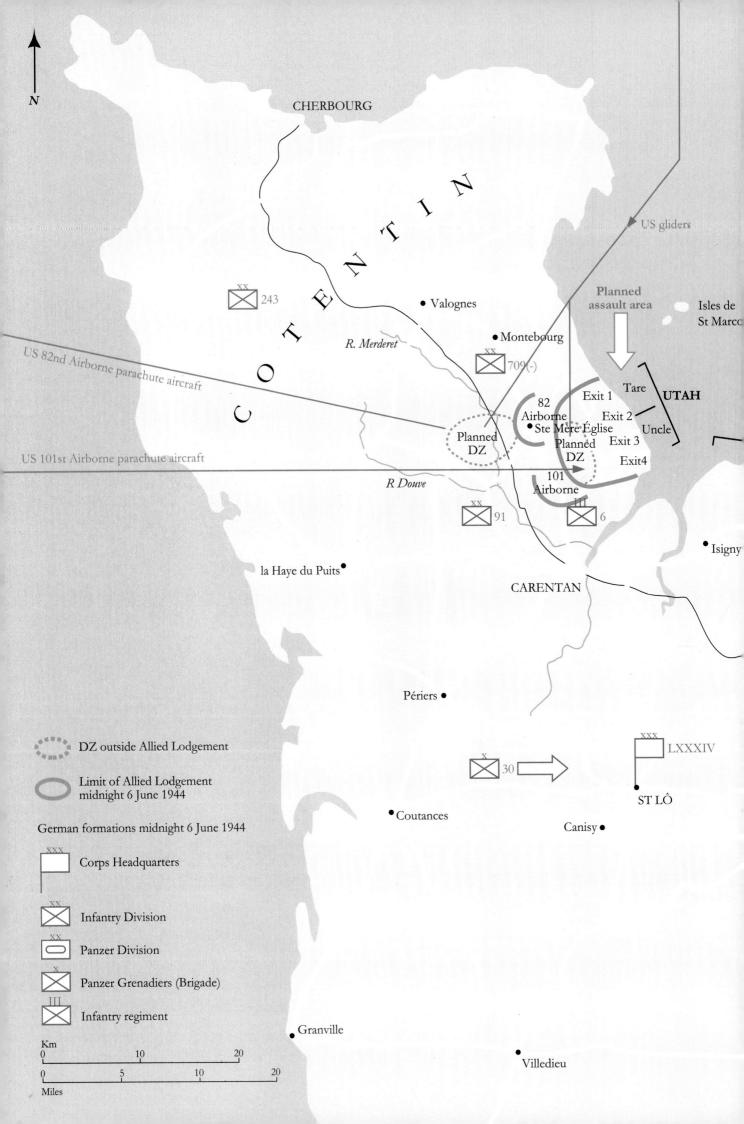

N

CHERBOURG

C O T E N T I N

• Valognes

243

R. Merderet

• Montebourg

709 (-)

Planned
assault area

Isles de
St Marco

US gliders

Exit 1   Tare

82
Airborne   Exit 2   **UTAH**
• Ste Mère Église   Uncle
Planned   Exit 3
DZ   Planned
DZ   Exit4

US 82nd Airborne parachute aircraft

Planned
DZ

US 101st Airborne parachute aircraft

R Douve

101
Airborne

91   6

• Isigny

la Haye du Puits •

CARENTAN

Périers •

30

LXXXIV

Coutances

ST LÔ

Canisy •

DZ outside Allied Lodgement

Limit of Allied Lodgement
midnight 6 June 1944

German formations midnight 6 June 1944

Corps Headquarters

Infantry Division

Panzer Division

Panzer Grenadiers (Brigade)

Infantry regiment

Km
0   10   20

0   5   10   20

Miles

• Granville

Villedieu •

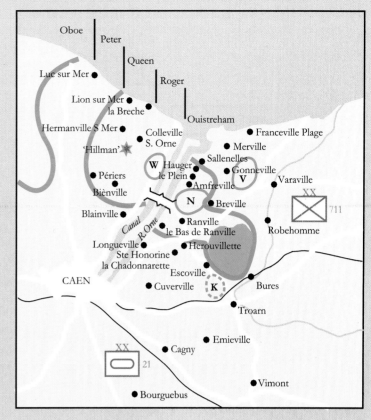

Oboe
Peter
Queen
Roger
Luc sur Mer
Lion sur Mer
la Breche
Ouistreham
Hermanville S Mer
Franceville Plage
Colleville
S. Orne
Merville
'Hillman'
Sallenelles
W Hauger
le Plein
V
Gonneville
Périers
Amfreville
Varaville
Biènville
N
Breville
Blainville
Ranville
le Bas de Ranville
Robehomme
Canal
R. Orne
Longueville
Herouvillette
Ste Honorine
la Chadonnarette
Escoville
K
Bures
CAEN
Cuverville
Troarn
Cagny
Emieville
XX 711
XX 21
Vimont
Bourguebus

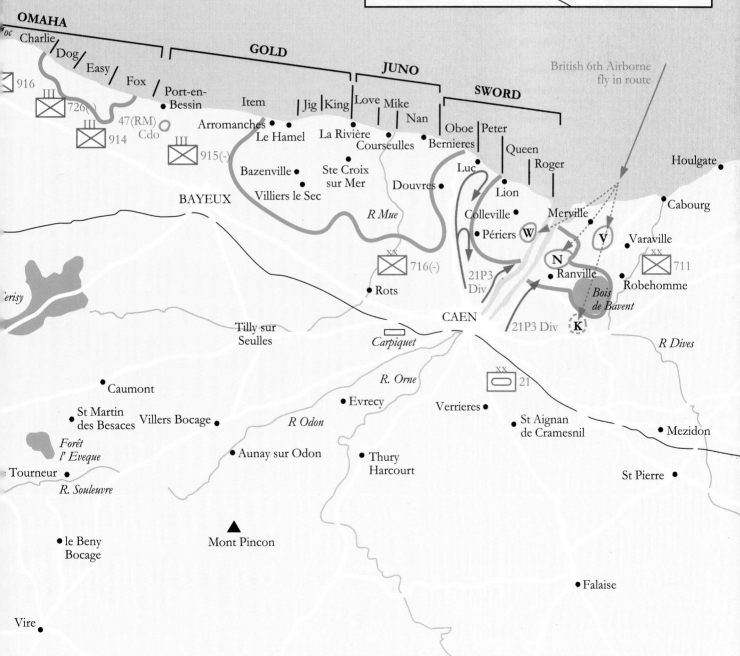

OMAHA
Charlie
Dog
Easy
Fox
GOLD
JUNO
SWORD
British 6th Airborne
fly in route
XX 916
Port-en-Bessin
Item
Jig King
Love Mike
Oboe Peter
916
III 726(-)
III 914
47(RM) Cdo
Arromanches
Le Hamel
La Rivière
Courseulles
Nan
Bernieres
Queen
Roger
Houlgate
III 915(-)
Bazenville
Ste Croix
sur Mer
Douvres
Luc
Cabourg
BAYEUX
Villiers le Sec
R Mue
Colleville
Périers
Lion
Merville
W
V
Varaville
XX 716(-)
N
XX 711
Rots
Ranville
Robehomme
21P3
Div
Bois
de Bavent
K
Tilly sur
Seulles
Carpiquet
21P3 Div
R Dives
erisy
CAEN
Caumont
R. Orne
St Martin
des Besaces
Villers Bocage
Evrecy
Verrieres
XX 21
Mezidon
Forêt
l' Eveque
R Odon
St Aignan
de Cramesnil
Tourneur
Aunay sur Odon
Thury
Harcourt
St Pierre
R. Souleuvre

le Beny
Bocage
Mont Pincon

Vire

Falaise

to Argentan

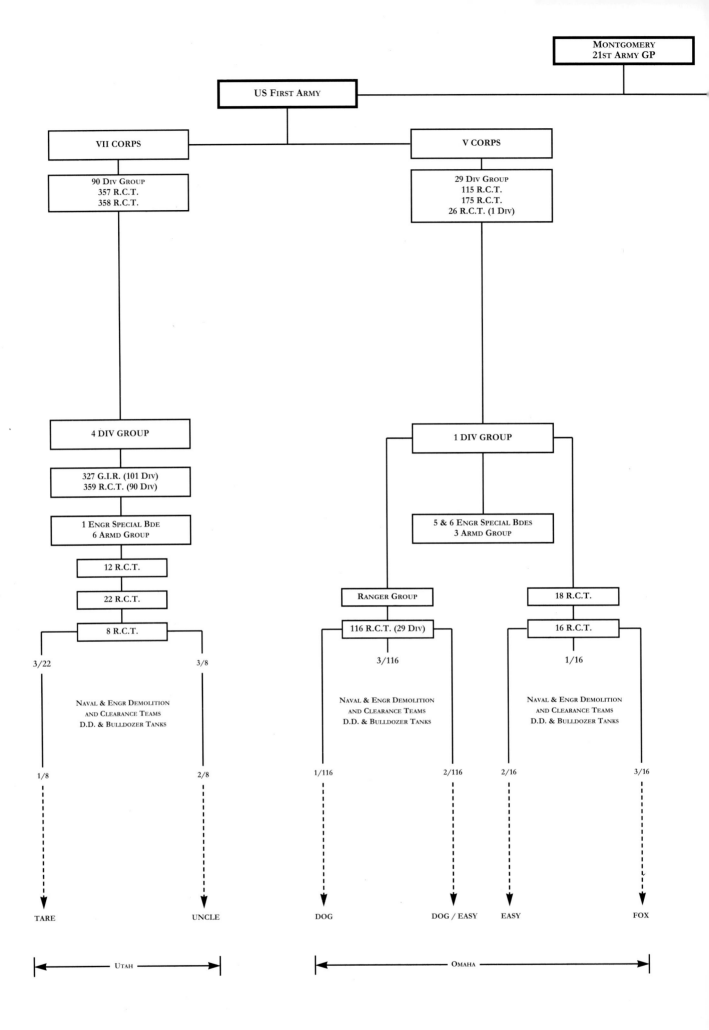

MONTGOMERY
21ST ARMY GP

US FIRST ARMY

VII CORPS

V CORPS

90 DIV GROUP
357 R.C.T.
358 R.C.T.

29 DIV GROUP
115 R.C.T.
175 R.C.T.
26 R.C.T. (1 DIV)

4 DIV GROUP

1 DIV GROUP

327 G.I.R. (101 DIV)
359 R.C.T. (90 DIV)

5 & 6 ENGR SPECIAL BDES
3 ARMD GROUP

1 ENGR SPECIAL BDE
6 ARMD GROUP

12 R.C.T.

22 R.C.T.

RANGER GROUP

18 R.C.T.

8 R.C.T.

116 R.C.T. (29 DIV)

16 R.C.T.

3/22   3/8

3/116

1/16

NAVAL & ENGR DEMOLITION
AND CLEARANCE TEAMS
D.D. & BULLDOZER TANKS

NAVAL & ENGR DEMOLITION
AND CLEARANCE TEAMS
D.D. & BULLDOZER TANKS

NAVAL & ENGR DEMOLITION
AND CLEARANCE TEAMS
D.D. & BULLDOZER TANKS

1/8   2/8

1/116   2/116   2/16   3/16

TARE   UNCLE

DOG   DOG / EASY   EASY   FOX

←——— UTAH ———→

←——————————— OMAHA ———————————→

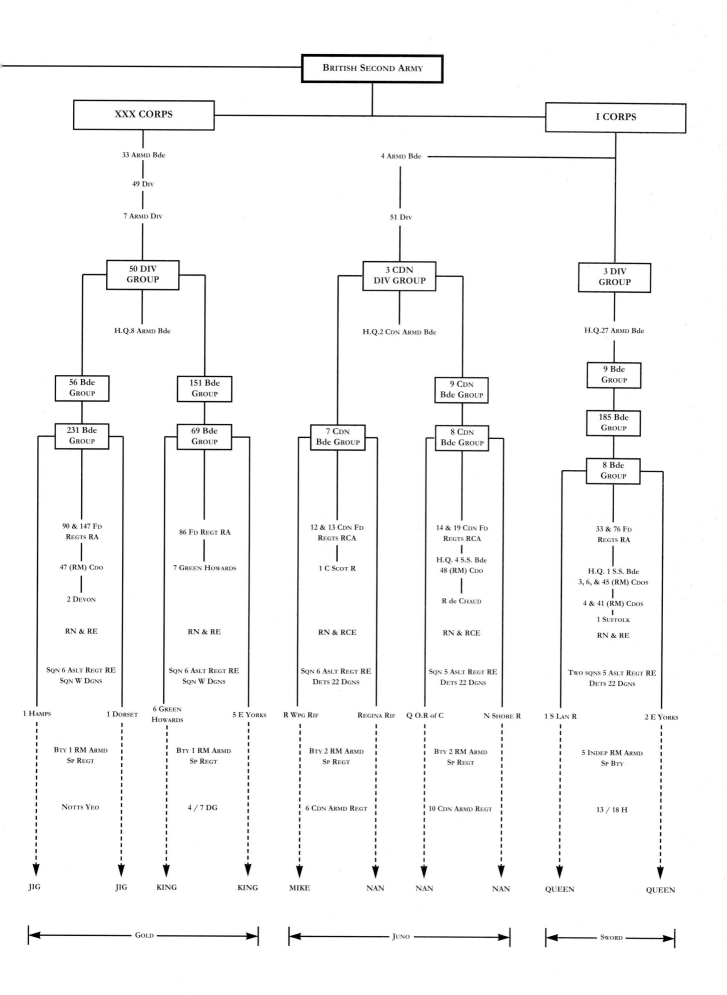

LANDING CRAFT

One of the great achievements of the Allies in the Second World War was the development of an array of specialised landing vessels for the projection of military power ashore. These were required by the ejection of the Allies from mainland Europe in 1940 and the need to return by sea. The British led the way in the concept of most types but the great invasion armada could not have been built without the enormous productive capacity of the United States. There were larger "landing ships" designed for ocean voyages and smaller "landing craft". Because of the short distances demanded by NEPTUNE, both larger and smaller types were usable for the cross-channel voyage.

Empire Halberd lowering craft in the lowering position off Gold beach.

61

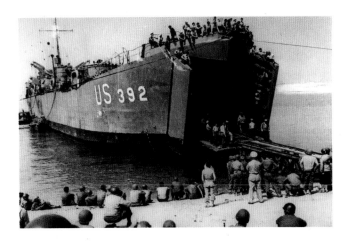

In order to carry infantry to the assault area and land them in small assault landing craft lowered over the side on davits, both the British and Americans deployed converted merchantmen, designated respectively infantry landing ships (LSI) and attack transports (APA). There were seven American APAs and three less specialised American transports (AP) fitted out as such.

The APAs carried 26 eight-ton Landing Craft Vehicle (LCV) and Personnel (LCVP) and two larger 23-ton Landing Craft Mechanised. Similar to the APAs were 18 British large infantry landing ships or LSI(L), some of which were American built. These carried 18-24 British type assault landing craft (LCA), slightly larger than the American LCVP at about 12 tons displacement. There were three medium infantry landing ships or LSI(M), one British (a former Dutch ferry) and two Canadian. These carried six LCA and two LCM each. There were six British Landing Ships Infantry (Small) all converted from 3,000-ton Belgian cross-channel ferries carrying eight LCA and 20 similar LSI(H) converted from British Channel and Irish Sea ferries with hand operated davits, usually for six LCA. Most of the LSI(H) retained merchant crews but the rest were commissioned as warships. The larger LSIs carried between 750 and 800 troops and the smaller ships about 200-500.

Landing ships that actually beached to land tanks and other vehicles were the Tank Landing Ships (LST). There were two types, the original British type converted from shallow draft oil tankers trading on the Maracaibo river in Venezuela, all three of which were used in NEPTUNE and the much more numerous American-built LST(2) , 59 of the latter, over half of those supplied to Britain under lend-lease, served under the White Ensign in the Normandy landings and 174 under the Stars and Stripes. The LST(2) was a diesel-powered ship almost 100 metres long and displacing over 2,000 tons loaded. It had been designed in the United States and had ballast tanks that allowed deep draft for ocean voyages and shallow draft for beaching. Maximum speed was 11.5 knots which gave it the nickname "large slow target". It could carry 20 Sherman tanks or up to 120 smaller vehicles. The bows of the ships had large double doors plus unloading ramp, and if beaching was impractical "Rhino" pontoon ferries could be used. LST were also used to lift smaller LCVP.

Tank landing craft (LCT) were little more than a quarter the displacement of LST. The standard British craft, the LCT(4) was almost 60 metres long and displaced almost 650 tons loaded. Diesel-engined it could make ten knots, and carry six-to-nine tanks landed through a hinged combined bow door and ramp. LCT lent themselves to numerous conversions as gunfire and rocket support vessels (see bombardment ships).

The Americans also mass-produced a rather smaller 300-ton vessel based on earlier British practice as the LCT (5) and (6). The American craft were smaller because of the need to transport them in larger vessels over oceanic distances. They could carry three-to-four tanks and were suitable both for cross-channel operations acting as a causeway between the LST and the shore. There were 350 LCT of all types with the Western Task Force and 487 with the Eastern.

Used widely by both Americans and British at Normandy was the 385-ton Large Infantry Landing Craft LCI(L) built to a 1942 British requirement as a vessel suitable for carrying up to 250 troops for 500 miles at 15 knots. All were built in America but 220 were supplied to the Royal navy under lend-lease. They were designed to beach with the troops going ashore down gangways on both sides of a conventional bow. LSI(L) were almost 50 metres long. There were 93 with the Western Task Force and 196 with the Eastern. In addition the British deployed with the latter, 39 LCI (Small), 110-ton 32-metre craft with a motor launch hull but able to carry over 100 troops.

Because of the short distances involved, very small landing craft normally only used for ship to shore transport were used for cross-channel runs. These included the 52-ton 15-metre long LCM able to carry one tank or 60 men and the 11-metre long LCP(L) (Large Landing Craft Personnel) as well as LCVP, like those carried by the APAs. The LCP(L) was a wooden craft built in the US to a British requirement for a vessel that could carry a complete platoon (30 troops); the LCVP was a modified, armed and armoured version designed to carry vehicles as well as personnel. It could carry three tons of vehicles or 36 men, landed through a hinged ramped bow.

The British had conceived of a large landing ship that would act as a mobile dock and carrier for smaller landing craft. The Landing Ships Dock (LSD) were not needed in the channel in their designed role but, two of the four supplied to the Royal Navy under lend-lease, *Northway* and *Oceanway*, were used off the beaches as landing craft repair ships. Other vessels pressed into service by the Royal Navy as Landing

Ships Emergency Repair (LSE) were the former minelayer *Adventure* and seaplane carrier *Albatross*.

A vital component of amphibious operations, the most complex of military actions, is effective command and control; and a number of specialised amphibious command ships, converted merchantmen with crammed communications equipment and facilities for a large staff were deployed in NEPTUNE.

Each British amphibious Task Force had a Landing Ship Headquarters (Large) a meduim-sized former armed merchant cruiser or armed boarding vessel (previously used in the blockade of Germany); HMS *Bululo* was with Task Force 'G', HMS *Hilary* with Task Force 'J' and HMS *Largs* with Task Force 'S'. The Navy had the Command Ship (AGC) the USS *Ancon* (a converted APA). In addition a number of converted British warships were used as Landing Ships Headquarters (Small) in command of amphibious groups within the British Task Forces. These included a former river gunboat, two Hunt class destroyers and five frigates. Converted LSI(L) were used in the British sector as Landing Craft Headquarters (LCH) for the local senior officers in the assault area. The Americans used similar Landing Craft Control (LCC) to control the movements of landing craft in their areas.

No less than 2,468 landing ships and craft (including fire support vessels) were allocated to the Eastern and Western Task Forces for the assault. Of these only 346 were operated by the US Navy or US Coast Guard. Manning the rest of this huge armada put a considerable strain on the increasingly overstretched manpower resources of the Royal Navy and Royal Marines. In addition, 1,656 more landing craft, barges trawlers and "Rhinos" were used as ship to shore ferries in the assault are as well as to assist damaged ships and craft. Losses were indeed significant. Between D-Day and D plus 30 some 26 LST were lost and no less than 307 LCT and 56 LCI.

The techniques of amphibious landing had however been triumphantly vindicated. Moreover, the tank landing ships and craft had laid the foundations for the roll-on, roll-off ferries that we take for granted today.

Opposite Left
LST unloading on the US Beaches after D-Day.
Opposite Right
Landing Craft Flak.
Below
LCTs bring in vehicles after D-Day.

A LOT HAS CHANGED-BUT THE WELCOME'S THE SAME.

N orthern Ireland was temporary home to thousands of WWii service personnel in its role as a major allied base. And every one of them took away some special recollection.

And Northern Ireland remembers them too, in a series of unique events, special museums and artifacts from that great struggle.

Among them are:

- D-Day Commemoration, Bangor, Co. Down 28th May - 5th June 1994.
- Anniversary of the U-Boat Fleet Surrender Londonderry 6th May 1995.
- Royal Ulster Rifles, Museum, Waring Street, Belfast.
- Castle Archdale, Flying Boat base, Co. Fermanagh

- Battle of the Atlantic Exhibition, the Tower Museum, Derry.
- Grey Point Coastal Defence Battery and Museum, Crawfordsburn, Co. Down.

So, whether you're re-living some memories, or wanting to know what it was really like, there's no better place than Northern Ireland.

Northern Ireland Tourist Board

St. Anne's Court, 59 North Street, Belfast BT1 1NB Tel: (0232) 246609
11 Berkeley Street, London W1X 5AD Tel: FREEPHONE 0800 282662
135 Buchanan Street, 1st Floor, Glasgow G1 2JA Tel: (041) 204 4454

50 years ago he risked everything for us. Now it's time to say thank you.

On 6th June 1944, D-Day, Norman Kirby risked his life so that we could live in freedom. Now he, and others like him, need you to fight for them.

Elderly people encounter many problems: poverty, cold, hunger, loneliness. But indifference means they often battle against them alone.

With your support Help the Aged can stop that happening.

Please give a donation today. The elderly men and women who lived through the war might not think they deserve our gratitude. But isn't it time we said 'thank you'?

Help the Aged, St. James's Walk, London EC1R 0BE.

D-DAY AND THE ROYAL ENGINEERS

The planning for D-Day began as early as 1941, involving the Royal Engineers from the very beginning. Information about possible landing places was gathered from all available sources, ranging from published travel guides to holiday postcards.

Special maps incorporating this information were drawn by Royal Engineer Surveyors. One of the many factors which influenced the selection of the landing areas was the suitability of the beaches for the assault, as well as the geology inland for the speedy construction of airfields. The latter information was provided by Royal Engineer geologists.

Checking the beaches and exits was the task of Combined Operations Pilotage Parties (COPPs), whose reconnaissance methods have been described elsewhere in this book. The Royal Engineers provided a number of the parties who engaged in these hazardous operations.

AIRBORNE ENGINEERS

The first Royal Engineers to land in France on D-Day, dropped with 6th Airborne Division just after midnight on 6th June 1944.
Their tasks were:-
● To assist in the seizure of the bridges over the Caen Canal and River Orne.

● If these bridges were blown, to assist in crossing the Canal and River Orne. For this task, a detachment of

Churchill AVRE with scissors bridge.

sappers with inflatable dinghies dropped with the 7th Parachute Battalion.

● To create a demolition belt on the River Dives, between Troarn and Varaville, including the destruction of the five road and rail bridges.

● To destroy the guns of the Merville Battery, under command of 9th Parachute Battalion.

● To clear glider landing zones (LZs) for glider-borne forces arriving just

before first light carrying divisional headquarters, anti-tank guns, and bulldozers. These LZs were to be extended and cleared of glider debris for the arrival of the main body of 6th Airlanding Brigade on the evening of D-Day.

With the exception of the operation at Merville, all these tasks were carried out successfully. The sapper troop responsible for the destruction of the guns of the Merville Battery was dropped over a wide area, and unable to join up with 9th Parachute Battalion. The Battery was temporarily neutralised by the 9th Battalion in the action described in the Chapter , 'By Air to Battle'.

ASSAULT FROM THE SEA

One of the stark messages from the unsuccessful Dieppe raid in 1942, was the need for armoured protection for the assault engineers who sustained heavy casualties while breaching the sea wall and other beach defences. Steps were taken to convert tanks into armoured vehicles suitable for this purpose. Eventually the Mark 3 and 4 versions of the Churchill tank were fitted with a Petard mortar with a calibre of 290 mm, which loaded from within the tank, fired up to four rounds a minute. The 40 lb Petard projectile, nicknamed the 'flying dustbin' because of its shape, carried a 26 lb demolition charge, and was accurate up to 80 yards. In addition two machine guns were carried, one in the turret, the other in the front of the hull.

Called the Armoured Vehicle Royal Engineers (AVRE), the basic version weighed 40 tons, and carried a crew of six: commander, driver, demolition engineer, wireless (radio) operator, mortar gunner and co-driver/Petard loader.

In late 1943, the 1st Assault Brigade Royal Engineers was formed as part of 79th Armoured division, which, under Major General Percy Hobart, had been given the task of co-ordinating the development of special armoured assault techniques and equipment.

Several variants of the AVRE were prominent in the leading waves of D-Day. Often referred to as 'Hobart's Funnies', they were invaluable for their effectiveness, versatility, and the protection they gave assault engineers working under heavy fire. The Americans declined the support of AVREs for their assaults, and paid the price, particularly on Omaha Beach.
The tasks carried out during the assault included:-
● The destruction of gun emplacements and defended buildings.

● The breaching of sea walls and other obstacles.

● The scaling of walls and the crossing of anti-tank ditches, bomb and shell craters.

● The laying of flexible matting, fascines and log carpets to provide firm going for tracked and wheeled vehicles.

● The placing of demolition charges for remote detonation.

● Destruction by Crocodile flamethrowers.

● Breaching of minefields and barbed wire by Bangalore Torpedo.

● Mineclearing with special ploughs.

Some of the special equipment carried by the AVREs is described in the box opposite

Each of the three leading infantry divisions assaulting the beaches in the British and Canadian sector; *Gold, Juno* and *Sword*, included two assault squadrons from 5th and 6th

Assault Engineer Regiments Royal Engineers. The primary tasks of the assault squadrons was to clear lanes across the beaches and to establish up to eight exits on to the first lateral road inland suitable for tracked vehicles.
Clearing the beaches involved:-
● Removing a wide variety of beach obstacles, exposed at low tide, to allow safe movement at high tide.

● Disarming and removing mines and other explosive devices from these obstacles.

Establishing beach exits involved:-
● Breaching sea walls, and creating and maintaining ramps and firm access routes through the soft sand above the high water line;
● Removing knocked-out vehicles obstructing beach exits.

All this had to be achieved under fire from buildings and pill-boxes on the sea front, and mortar and artillery fire from further inland. Each assault squadron was equipped with AVREs. In addition the assault teams included a number of Sherman Crabs from 30th Armoured Brigade. These Shermans mounted a rotary chain flail on the front of the tank to destroy mines in its path, thus clearing lanes up the beach. The AVREs then attacked the first line of beach defences with their Petard mortars, while more sappers landed to continue the clearance of the beaches.

FASCINES
Fascines consisting of bundles of brushwood for crossing ditches, craters and similar obstacles, were carried on the front of the AVRE on a specially designed cradle, and could be jettisoned from inside.

ASSAULT BRIDGING
The Standard Box Girder assault bridges carried by some AVREs were placed against sea walls enabling armoured vehicles to surmount them, or placed over shell or bomb craters, anti-tank ditches, and natural obstacles such as small rivers. If necessary another AVRE would drop a fascine at the foot of the obstacle to provide a base on which to rest forward end of the bridge. If an obstacle with a drop on both sides had to be crossed, a third AVRE dropped another fascine on the far side to cushion the fall of armoured vehicles crossing.

MAT-LAYING DEVICES
A variety of systems were evolved to lay flexible surfaces over poor ground, or where much traffic was concentrated, such as a breach in a wall or minefield or on the approach to a bridge on an unsurfaced track. These included:

1) LOG CARPET: This consisted of a carpet of up to 100 logs, each 14 feet long, with an average diameter of 6-8 inches, laid side-by-side, and joined by a wire rope passing through each log. The carpet was carried on a steel frame, mounted above the AVRE turret, and held in place with wire lashings at the forward end. After positioning the AVRE small charges were fired to cut these cables, and the first section of the carpet fell towards the ground. The weight of this pulled further logs off the frame, onto the ground in front of the AVRE, which drove forward over the logs until the entire carpet unrolled. Depending on the diameter of the logs, the carpet could be up to 80 feet long.

2) BOBBIN: Reconnaissance before D-Day revealed strips of clay on some parts of the beaches. To overcome the possibility of vehicles bogging down in these areas, a flexible carpet laying AVRE was designed. This carried a Bobbin consisting of a large steel drum, carried on two support arms fixed to the sides of the AVRE, with a carpet made of hessian reinforced with scaffolding tubes across its width rolled round the drum. To lay the carpet, the Bobbin was lowered over the front of the AVRE, allowing the hessian to start unreeling. As the AVRE moved forward, it ran onto the carpet, which continued to unreel until laid. These carpets were satisfactory for wheeled traffic, but could not stand up to tracked vehicles for long.

Below
Concrete Phoenixes and lighters, part of Mulberry harbour in England before D-Day.
Bottom Right
Mulberry Harbour, the first part of the floating causeway that connected the Whale pierheads with the shore, coming to the beach at Arromanches.

All the while, infantry were moving through the growing bridgehead. Further support was given by Duplex Drive (DD) tanks of the Royal Armoured Corps. Several beach exits were opened within an hour of landing, allowing armour to move inland.

As the tide rose, the beach area became smaller, and obstacles which had not been removed or destroyed became hazards for succeeding waves of landing craft. Beach clearance continued in conjunction with naval specialists in underwater explosives. As the bridgehead expanded, the tasks for Sappers inland increased, such as mine-clearance followed by mine-laying to secure captured positions against German counter-attacks, and removal of inland obstacles. The price piaed for success was heavy. In some sectors up to 50 per cent of the specialised armour was knocked out, with many casualties among the crews. But the landings had been achieved, and the build-up of troops and vehicles across the beaches continued steadily until the completion of the first section of the Mulberry Harbour offered an easier and safer way of getting ashore.

69

MULBERRY - A HARBOUR GOES TO FRANCE

There were two Mulberry Harbours, both of British design and construction; Mulberry A off the American sector and Mulberry B off the British sector. A Sapper, Colonel S. K. Gilbert, commanded the port construction force for Mulberry B, with Lieutenant Colonel R. Mais RE, later Lord Mayor of London, responsible for the pierheads and roadways. When the various parts of Mulberry had crossed the channel, by tow, under their own steam, or in shipping, construction began. By 9th June, 1,500 feet of the centre pier and 600 feet of the east pier had been completed.

During the morning of 19th June a fierce storm blew up, continuing until the night of 22nd June, with waves up to 14 feet high. When the sea abated, the debris at Mulberry A was piled high on the beach, and the harbour was so badly damaged it was abandoned. Equipment salvaged from Mulberry A was used to repair Mulberry B, which continued operations until the Port of Antwerp was opened at the end of November 1944; considerably longer than the 90-day period of operation originally envisaged; a tribute to the designers of Mulberry, and those responsible for its construction and maintenance.

In addition to the tasks already described, which were carried out in all the battles of the campaign, until the end of the War in Europe, the Royal Engineers responsibilities included:-

- Air Strip and Air Field construction.

- Bridging and rafting.

- Roadworks.

- Water Supply.

- Fuel pipelines, including the Pipe Line Under the Ocean PLUTO, which pumped fuel direct form England to Normandy.

Truly the Royal Engineers lived up to their two mottoes: *'Ubique'*, and *'Quo Fas and Gloria Ducunt'* - 'Everywhere', and 'Where Right and Glory Lead'.

Left
Mulberry Harbour, trucks driving over a causeway at low tide.
Below
Sappers building a Bailey bridge on pontoons over the Caen Canal.

THE ROYAL ARMOURED CORPS ON D-DAY

On 1st April 1939, just five months before the Germans invaded Poland, the Royal Armoured Corps was formed by amalgamating the original Royal Tank Corps with the existing mechanised cavalry and yeomanry regiments.

The Corps expanded rapidly over the next five years and it was a well tempered, armoured spearhead that pierced Hitler's Atlantic Wall and led the Allied forces into occupied France.

Although tanks had taken part in earlier amphibious operations such as Madagascar and Sicily, the authorities were cautious about relying too heavily on them in the initial stages of a landing since the unfortunate experience of Dieppe in the summer of 1942.

Now, however, their importance had been re-appraised, their capabilities enhanced and the techniques for handling them thoroughly explored and practised.

On the British and Canadian beaches they were regarded as the key to success and they lived up to expectations.

Before taking a closer look at them perhaps we should take a moment to remember that many of the British soldiers who crossed the Channel that day had never seen action before. After a rough crossing in flat-bottomed boats

Main Picture
A Humber light reconnaissance car during training somewhere in England.

these men, understandably apprehensive, were plunged straight into a mayhem of violence, danger and death from which they emerged as accomplished veterans; a tribute to the high standard of their training.

The British tanks which landed on 6th June 1944 may be divided into three categories; specialised armour, conventional tanks, and special forces.

The term Specialised Armour describes those tanks which had been modified to perform specific roles in the assault, in addition to their normal fighting capabilities. On D-Day most of these special tanks were controlled by the unique 79th Armoured Division. Many were operated by the Royal

Engineers, whose achievements are recorded elsewhere, but Royal Armoured Corps regiments were responsible for two specific functions.

First among these, and theoretically first ashore, were the Sherman DD, or Duplex Drive, swimming tanks devised by the Hungarian engineer Nicholas Straussler. Each tank was enclosed by a boat-shaped canvas screen, tall enough to make it buoyant, and powered in the water by a pair of marine propellers, driven off the tracks. Launched from landing craft at anything up to 5,000 yards from the shore, they looked innocuous enough in the water, like small, collapsible boats, but once their tracks bit into the Normandy sand the screens came down and they went into

action, like any other tanks, supporting the infantry right from the water's edge.

In practice it didn't go quite like that. Three RAC regiments operated DD tanks in addition to the Canadians and Americans. Of these the 13th/18th Hussars was the only regiment able to stick to the original plan. Their War Diary records that they had been sailing for over 17 hours in rough seas before they arrived on station.

A and B Squadrons launched from their anchored landing craft about 5,000 yards off Queen Beach in 3rd Infantry Division's sector and, despite some mishaps, the majority got ashore and provided valuable support. Meanwhile C Squadron and Regimental HQ, in

Top
A Tetrach light tank of 6th Airborne Reconnaissance Regiment emerging from a Hamilcar glider, during training.
Middle
Two Sherman Crab flail tanks and Churchills re-embaking in a Landing Crraft Tank (LCT), after a practice on a Norfolk beach.
Bottom
A Daimler armoured car equipped for wading during training for D-Day.

73

conventional Shermans, landed at La Breche a little to the east where they found the beach 'like Piccadilly Circus in the rush hour' but managed to capture both their objectives by early evening. Further west, around La Riviere, the 4th/7th Dragoon Guards were due to launch B and C Squadrons, with A Squadron landing dry.

In the end, owing to the weather conditions, it was agreed that the landing craft should take all the tanks right in to the beach, which they duly did. The regiment came up against tough opposition and even took some casualties from friendly fire but by midnight they regrouped and settled down for the night.

The third DD regiment was the Sherwood Rangers (Nottinghamshire Yeomanry). They were to land on the British right, between Le Hamel and La Riviere. B and C Squadrons finally launched within a few hundred yards of the beach and virtually drove ashore through the breakers, in which they lost eight tanks from drowning and others to enemy fire.

A Squadron arrived shortly afterwards but, between congestion on the beaches and villages reduced to rubble inland they experienced some difficulty in supporting their infantry. However by evening A Squadron, with a battalion of the Essex Regiment, was not far short of Bayeaux.

Following the DD tanks were Sherman Crabs. This code name disguised those tanks fitted with rotary, mine-clearing flails which, on D-Day were operated by two RAC regiments, the Westminster Dragoons and the 22nd Dragoons.

B and C Squadrons of the former worked with the British 50th Infantry Division on the right, while A Squadron, 22nd Dragoons supported British 3rd Infantry Division on the left and B Squadron was in the middle, with 3rd Canadian Division. The Crabs could not swim ashore. They were first water-proofed in Britain and this allowed them to wade through shallow water, from the point where their landing craft grounded, to dry land. Another thing they could not do was flail and fight at the same time.

For one thing mine-clearing required a great deal of concentration and, for another, the amount of dirt thrown up by the flail chains, not to mention exploding mines, made it virtually impossible to see anything. In any case fighting was a last resort.

Their value as mine-clearers required that they should not be risked in combat more than absolutely essential although, on the day, they often had to support infantry with gunfire until the DD tanks arrived and some Crabs scored notable successes against formidable enemy weapons. The flails did their best work behind the beaches, clearing the lateral roads and opening up communications to strengthen the bridgehead.

The 141st Regiment RAC (The Buffs) also operated specialised armour but not, then, as part of 79th Armoured Division. They were equipped with Crocodiles - Churchill tanks towing trailers and equipped with fearsome flamethrowers.

The regiment contributed two troops from C Squadron which sailed from Southampton to come ashore at Le Hamel and La Riviere respectively. The former lost all three tanks on the beach but 13 Troop managed to get two into action although they seem to have functioned mainly as gun tanks on that first day.

The conventional elements of the RAC committed on D-Day were two Sherman regiments and one squadron of armoured cars. This was C Squadron, The Inns of Court Regiment. The task set for this small force seems almost impossible in retrospect, and many believed it to be so at the time. They were to land from two LCTs near Graye-sur-Mer in the Canadian sector and them move inland by a variety of routes to take and destroy up to six bridges in order to prevent a counterattack by 21st Panzer Division. One landing craft sank just short of the beach and its vehicles did not get into action until later in the day. The other landing craft got its ramp down and disgorged the remaining armoured demolition equipment.

They got clear of the beach after some effort but the rest of the day was spent in a series of costly skirmishes and none of the bridges were taken before dusk, although some cars were then as much as 11 miles from the beaches.

The two Sherman regiments were the East Riding Yeomanry and Staffordshire Yeomanry. The former, which had been a Royal Tank Corps armoured car company before the war, originally trained on DD tanks but handed these over to the Canadians and reverted to the normal kind in the previous winter.

They were late getting ashore, and later still breaking clear of the beach area near Ouistreham. They then proceeded to a designated assembly area where, at the touch of a button, the waterproofing gear was blown off their tanks.

From here they moved through Hermanville and Colville to spend the night on high ground overlooking the Orne river.

The landing craft of the Staffordshire Yeomanry touched down west of Ouistreham in the wake of the 13th/18th Hussars about mid-morning. A Squadron soon got involved in mopping up actions but the other two, with C well ahead and their Stuart reconnaissance tanks out in front, began a promising advance in the direction of Caen.

Reports were soon received of enemy tanks advancing rapidly into the area so the regiment regrouped in the area of Hill 61. Here they met the advance elements of 21st Panzer Division making their long expected counterattack and drove them off with sufficient losses to guarantee the landing beaches for that first, vital night.

The special forces mentioned earlier are not, perhaps, the kind we mean today, but rather units detailed for special tasks which are difficult to categorise any other way. There were three with RAC connections, all very different in style, purpose and equipment.

First the Reconnaissance Corps, which had been absorbed into the RAC in January 1944. The 3rd Recce Regiment had

some elements ashore on D-Day for what were described as 'beach duties' while the 61st Regiment contributed two squadrons for its traditional role.

Equipped with light reconnaissance cars, little more than armoured private cars, it undertook reconnaissance duties at divisional level. Mention should also be made of the associated GHQ Liaison Regiment - Phantom- which did the same kind of thing at Corps level.

Affiliated to the Royal Armoured Corps through its connections with the Recce Corps, Phantom operated patrols in Jeeps and armoured White scout cars along the entire Allied front, reporting back direct to Corps HQ in England. Removed from all the normal responsibilities of combat troops, its highly-trained teams kept the high command fully informed of developments as they happened, independent of normal channels.

One of the strangest tanks forces to hit the beach on 6th June was the Royal Marines Armoured Support Group. Equipped with outdated Centaur close support tanks its original role had been to remain on board landing craft and provide fire support for the Royal Marine Commandos.

In the event, General Montgomery decided that they should go ashore, so, with drivers supplied from the RAC, they landed at a number of points and did valuable work since their 95mm howitzers proved very effective against enemy pill-boxes and gun emplacements. The Canadian Official History is particularly complimentary about them.

Finally there was one RAC regiment that did not use landing craft at all. This was 6th Airborne Reconnaissance

Regiment which arrived in Hamilcar gliders, towed by Halifax bombers, late in the evening of D-Day.

Their task was to support General Gale's 6th Airborne Division which had dropped astride the Orne river and Caen Canal before dawn to cover the left flank of the entire Allied bridgehead. The regiment was equipped with Tetrarch light tanks, carried one per glider.

Their performance was disappointing because most of the tanks got stray parachute lines tangled around their tracks and could not move until the next day, but their arrival had an unexpected consequence. The gliders, including the Hamilcars carrying the Tetrachs, appeared overhead just as 21st Panzer was slogging it out with the Staffordshire Yeomanry, and that was too much for the Germans. Convinced they were about to be cut off, and already battling against strong opposition, they turned about and headed back for Caen while they still could.

Main Picture
A Sherman in Normandy by a Horsa Glider.
Inset
Shermans driving inland, Normandy.

The Beaches near Lion-sur-Mer, Normandy 1944 by Edward Ardizzone
© Imperial War Museum London

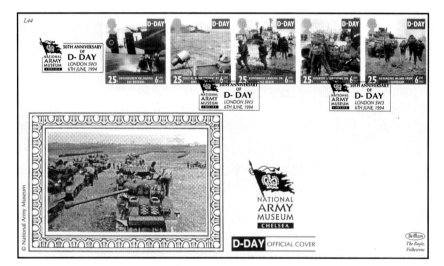

Fifty years ago, the World's greatest invasion changed the course of history. To commemorate the D-Day Anniversary on 6th June, the leading designers of First Day Covers in Great Britain have combined with the two major military museums, the Imperial War Museum and the National Army Museum, to produce two beautiful and evocative limited edition First Day Covers, which will be treasured by discerning collectors.

On D-Day 1994, 175,000 allied troops invaded France along a 70 mile stretch of coastline. It was the most critical day of the Second World War. In the horror of the shells, bombs and tracer bullets, many thousands of brave soldiers died but, at the end of the day, the beaches were secured and the tide of war had turned.

MAJOR NATIONAL MUSEUMS

Both the National Army Museum and the Imperial War Museum are staging major exhibitions , and both are essential viewing to understand the full impact of the D-Day.

UNIQUE POSTMARKS

Both of these covers have a Benham designed Royal Mail postmark to be applied on one day only, 6th June . Both covers cost £5.50 plus 50p postage and packing.

MONEY-BACK GUARANTEE

Needless to say, both of these covers carry a full money-back guarantee if not absolutely delighted.

Act now, as demand will almost certainly exceed supply. We can only accept orders for maximum of three sets per order. Send in your order today to avoid disappointment, either by returning this application, or by telephoning 071 354 5566.

Dear Dave,

Last week I got well and truly plastered.

I really landed myself in it this time. Who'd have thought I could break my leg after parachuting for ten years? Sarge reckons I should join the Navy...

Royal Mail
International

AN AIRMAIL LETTER MAKES A WORLD OF DIFFERENCE

ARTILLERY SUPPORT

The role of the Gunners on D-Day was to find the enemy on the ground and in the air and then destroy him during the assault, the build-up and the break-out and to destroy counter-attacks.

During the assault 7th and 33rd Field Regiments of 3rd (British) Division, 12th and 13th of 3rd (Canadian) Division and 86th (Hertfordshire Yeomanry) and 90th (City of London) Field Regiments of 50th (British) Division were part of the naval and aerial bombardment as the lead assault waves closed on the beaches. These six regiments produced 144 self propelled 25-pounder Sextons or 105mm Priests for the run-in shoot, with a troop of four guns allotted to one landing craft.

Firing started at 0655 hours on 6th June at a range of 11,000 yards. Each LCT captain held his craft steady on bearing while the Gunners reduced range as they closed. Firing continued to 3,000 yards and a total of 9,360 rounds were fired. The effect on the enemy was devastating and many of the defenders were killed, wounded or dazed as the leading infantry landed.

Captain Robert Kiln of 86th Regiment: *"By now we were only 2,000 yards from the shore, I had perfect view of our shells falling on their targets at La Riviere and on the wireless I could hear George Loveday and Ted Hall on the air observing and correcting the firing from their speedboats in front of us. Wireless perfect, weather bloody ....."*

Captain JP Cook of 90th Field Regiment said as his landing craft approached the beach: *"Suddenly out of the smoke appeared the coast line and then the rocket ships let their salvoes go, it didn't look as if much could survive, all good for morale."* He landed his tank and immediately called for fire, first from (a Marine battery) armed with Centaurs (Cromwell tanks fitted with 95 mm guns) but so far they had failed to get ashore. So he called on his own guns still at sea. As the action continued he brought in the fire of two destroyers and finally back to his own regiment, by then coming into action on the beach.

Main Picture
A 5.5 inch medium gun being loaded.
Middle
40mm Bofors guns of 51st Highland Division coming ashore, 24th June 1944
Left
A self-propelled Priest with crew digging in.

The Gunners of 213rd Airlanding Light Battery had already landed by glider with their 75 mm pack howitzers close to the Orne Bridges and were in action. Meanwhile Forward Observing Officers (FOOs) and Naval Gunfire Support Officers (NGSOs) were landing with the leading assault companies.

The guns themselves started to land at 0825 hours. Lieutenant Colonel Nigel Tapp commanding 7th Field Regiment of 3rd (BR) Division was ashore by 0830 hours at Hermanville on Sword Beach. He said:

"As we landed the whole area was packed with armoured vehicles. The guns of my regiment were unable to get off the beach so they came into action on the waters edge The houses screened them so most of the enemy shells hit the houses or passed overhead into the sea. As the tide was coming in the guns edged further up the beach.".

By 0800 hours guns of 20th and 102nd Anti-Tank Regiments were ashore and in action with their 17-pounders on Sword and Gold Beaches respectively. Captain Perring Thomas B Troop of 41st Battery, 20th Regiment equipped with self-propelled 17-pounder M10s broke out of the beaches at 1315 hours and set off along 185th Brigade's axis. They soon met German tanks and after losing one gun they destroyed their first two Panzers. By last light they were in the orchards west of Bieville with 2nd KSLI.

During the run-in, the anti-aircraft Gunners of 127th, 139th and 320th Battery of 93rd LAA Regiments with their 40mm Bofors, 20mm guns and 0.5-inch machine guns protected the non-naval ships of the invasion fleet and later, the great floating pontoons of the Mulberry Harbour. The guns of 25th and 93rd LAA regiments were ashore on Sword and Gold Beaches respectively by noon 6th June.

They were followed by the 3.7-inch heavy guns of 103rd HAA Regiment which had two guns ashore by last light and was credited with two kills. But enemy air activity on D-Day was smaller than expected. Nevertheless six Bofors of F Troop 93rd Regiment downed 17 enemy aircraft in the first six days.

Two SP Bofors of this regiment were in action on the Orne bridges by late afternoon and as they were coming into action shot down two Me 109s. One of the problems in the anti-air battle was control of air space. Very tight rules of engagement were enforced limiting gun fire to under 3,000 feet and then only on positively identified targets. During the assault control was exercised from ships.

The main job of 76th Field Regiment of 3rd (BR) Division was to get ashore and into action to cover the tiny and vulnerable bridgehead on the Orne. Four subalterns of the 76th jumped with the parachute assault to act as FOOs for this operation; one fell wide, one was captured but the remaining two soon had contact with the regiment and were able to bring fire to bear.

On Gold Beach a gun of 147th Field Regiment, by then ashore with the second wave, ripped out a nest of snipers and machine guns at Le Hamel at point blank range, while 90th Field regiment destroyed four German 88mm guns which were holding up the advance. It was at 1500 hours that

Captain JP Cook of 90th Regiment joined up with the 1st Dorsets for their attack on Puits d' Herode at 1500 hours. *"I ranged a troop and gave the target 40 rounds as the attack went in. The guns were beautifully together and the infantry were close to the bursting shells and took the position without loss giving them great confidence. A small counter-attack developed in our rear but our guns soon dealt with it. By evening we met up with the Devons on Ryes Ridge and arranged defensive fire tasks. I looked across at the colossal armada off the beaches, an unforgettable sight in the setting sun."*

FOOs were moving inland directing naval and artillery fire and breaking up local counter-attacks. Battery commanders were alongside battalion commanders, regimental commanding officers alongside brigade commanders and Commanders Royal Artillery (CRAs) alongside divisional commanders. This system ensured maximum co-ordination of fire with manoeuvre at all levels.

As more and more guns came ashore, their fire was concentrated where it was most needed. Colonel Tapp on Sword Beach again: *"Everyone was cheering and the sun was shining as 7th Field Regiment passed through Hermanville at 1200 hours on that memorable day to come into action alongside the leading infantry. A battery of 122mm guns was holding them up near Perriers so Major Rae went off a company of KSLI and with our gunfire silenced them. We were again held up by the strong position at 'Hillman' just south of Colville which we engaged with everything we had. At last light we were counter-attacked by about a dozen Mark IV tanks but we beat these off."*

Lieutenant Colonel George Fanshaw commanding 86th Regiment on Gold Beach was ashore early and reports the complete success of Phase 1 - 5th Green Howards had taken Mont Fleury Lighthouse; 6th Green Howards had taken Mont Fleury Battery and Ver-sur-Mer fell to 7th Green Howards so clearing all ground overlooking the beaches. By 0900 hours 86th Field Brigade and all in some 90 minutes. Then off for Phase 2.

Stephen Perry, FOO with 7th Green Howards for their attack on Creully bridge:
"...... a lot of Jerries were having a go at us from over the river, so here goes, 'Troop Target' ..... and a perfect shoot comes down slap on top them; 'Just the job', says the company commander."

One of the problems on D-Day was that of finding enemy guns. Air photographs ended up in Odiham in Hampshire but a powerful wireless link had been established to pass locations direct to HQRAs ashore. This worked well and the enemy guns were then subjected to heavy bombardment.

So by the end of D-Day the Gunners had some six field, two anti-tank and two LAA regiments, an air landing light battery and both HQRAs ashore and in action. Fire was already being co-ordinated and concentrated where it was most needed. Already several counter-attacks had been broken up. Co-ordination of fire with movement was developing fast. The omens were better than they had dared to hope.

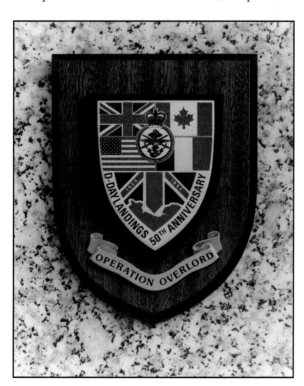

UTAH BEACH

THE UNITED STATES
AIRBORNE DIVISIONS
AND VIITH CORPS

A campaign study by the United States War Department quotes Colonel Van Fleet, the Commanding Officer of the 8th Infantry Regiment, reporting to the Commander of the United States 4th Infantry Division at 1025 on 6th June 1944, after landing on Utah Beach: *'Everything is going OK'*, and at midnight: *'Defense (sic) is not stubborn'*

The comparatively trouble-free progress inland from Utah Beach of the 4th Infantry Division, the leading division of VIIth Corps, was made possible by the United States 82nd and 101st Airborne Divisions, which had dropped inland of the beachhead, some five hours before the seaborne assault began.

Infantry on Utah Beach.

After landing on Utah Beach, the objectives of Major General 'Lightning Joe' Collins' United States VIIth Corps were to cut the entire Cotentin Peninsula at its base, before driving north to seize the port of Cherbourg. The Germans had flooded the low ground behind the beaches and the valleys of the Douve and Merderet Rivers, the dominant terrain features of the

Peninsula. The only exits from Utah Beach were four causeways crossing flooded land.

Bridges and causeways over the two rivers, and the surrounding inundations, provided the only crossing points for enemy counter-attacks on the beachhead from the west and south-west, and would also be needed by VIIth Corps to break out.

There was a danger that troops landing on Utah Beach might be hemmed in on the coast either by the lagoon-like area behind the beach, or by the flooded river valleys. So General Montgomery decided that airborne troops must secure the beach exits and river crossings, overruling Air Chief Marshal Leigh-Mallory, the Commander-in-Chief Allied Expeditionary Air Forces, who predicted up to 80 per cent losses in aircraft and gliders to German flak. The 82nd Airborne Division was to secure the western edge of the VIIth Corps bridgehead, by capturing St Mere-Eglise, a key communications centre, and establish deep bridgeheads over the Merderet, on the two main roads westward from St Mere-Eglise. The 101st Airborne Division was to clear the way for the seaborne assault by seizing the western exits of the four causeways from the beach across the inundated area. At the same time the Division was to establish defensive arcs along the northern and southern edges of the invasion area, and establish bridgeheads across the River Douve at two points for later exploitation in a drive south to Carentan to link up with U.S Vth Corps advancing from Omaha Beach. Both divisions were to drop between 01:15 and 01:30 on D-Day, about an hour after their comrades-in-arms, the British 6th Airborne Division, on the eastern flank of the Normandy lodgement area.

The paratroop elements of the 82nd and 101st Airborne Divisions, consisting of six regiments, each of three battalions, with parachute field artillery and engineers, numbered more than 13,000 men. This force was flown from airfields in southern England in 925 C-47s. An additional 4,000 men consisting of glider infantry with supporting weapons, medical and signal units was to arrive in 500 gliders on D-Day and on D plus 1.

Both divisions, like their British counterparts, were preceded by pathfinders dropping some 30 minutes ahead of the main force, to mark the Dropping Zones (DZs), and the Landing Zones (LZs), for the gliders.

As the aircraft carrying the 101st Airborne Division approached the French coast, they flew into scattered cloud and haze, and began to break formation. In accordance with American practice, only the leader in each group of aircraft had a qualified navigator. To have a chance of finding the correct DZ, each pilot had to keep dead on course. On crossing the coast, German flak guns opened up, and many pilots, contrary to orders, took violent evasive action. Many of the parachute soldiers standing, waiting to jump, in the rolling aircraft were thrown to the floor, and were struggling to get up again when the green 'go' light came on. Sticks were slow exiting, and were widely scattered on landing.

The difficulties facing the aircrew were greatly increased by most of the Division's pathfinders dropping some distance from the assigned DZs, so the beacons were not correctly

located. Sticks were dropped all over the Cherbourg peninsula, some as far as 20 miles away.

The drop was a shambles, although better than that of the 82nd Airborne Division. Of the 6,600 parachute soldiers of the 101st, about, 1,500 were either killed or captured on landing, and about 60 per cent of the Division's equipment was lost in containers dropped in swamps, or in fields covered by enemy fire.

There were also numerous casualties in many of the gliders, landing before first light. Many crashed in the tiny fields in that part of Normandy; much smaller than the rolling cornfields astride the River Orne and Caen Canal, used as LZs by the majority of the gliders supporting the British 6th Airborne Division. Among the dead was the assistant commander of 101st Airborne Division, strapped into the passenger seat of his jeep, he broke his neck when his glider crashed into a bank.

Despite these losses, and the ensuing chaos, the 101st Airborne Division, in company with its sister divisions the 82nd and British 6th Airborne, fulfilled the majority of its tasks. Even if, according to the United States War Department campaign study: 'many of the missions carried out were undertaken by mixed groups which did not correspond with original assignments'. Fortunately, the Germans were confused by the scattered drop, and being unable to fully comprehend the size and scope of the invasion, reacted slowly.

The experiences of Lieutenant Robert Cole's 3rd Battalion, 502nd Parachute Infantry were typical of many that night. His task; to secure the two northerly beach exits, numbers 3 and 4. An hour after landing he had found 30 men, some of his own battalion, and others from the 501st Regiment and the 82nd Division. After killing and capturing a German column travelling in vehicles, he met some of the 2nd Battalion who had discovered that their objective, a battery, had been abandoned Having despatched his strays to find their own units, he divided the remainder into two parties, to seize the two exits. By 07:30, both groups were in place without having encountered any opposition, and in a good position to deal with enemy withdrawing in front of 4th Infantry Division advancing from the beach. At last light, the battalion, by now 250 strong, as soldiers trickled in, was ordered to form the divisional reserve for operations the following day. Cole was to be awarded the Congressional Medal of Honour for his part in the battle round Carentan some days later, and was killed at Eindhoven during Operation Market Garden that September.

Ten minutes after the 101st's aircraft became airborne, the leading wave of the 82nd took off in the C-47s of 52nd Troop Carrier Command. With the leading wave, headed for DZ O north-west of St Mere-Eglise, was Major General Matthew B Ridgway, the commander of the 82nd. Like Major General Maxwell Taylor, commanding the 101st, he had never completed a formal parachute course. Indeed, Taylor's drop into Normandy was his fifth jump, and qualified him for his parachute wings. Lieutenant Colonel Vandervoort commanding the 2nd Battalion 505 Parachute Infantry, lead jumpmaster for his battalion, was standing in the door of the leading aircraft, checking each landmark as they passed overhead. The green light came on in his aircraft, but he could see that they had

United States Infantry in southern England waiting to embark.

not yet crossed the river Merderet. If he jumped, American practice dictated that the navigator in his aircraft would flash a green light from his astrodome, to signal every other aircraft to switch on their green lights. Vandervoort ordered the Air Corps crew chief, standing beside him, to tell the pilot over the intercom to switch off the green light. Soon the lights of the 'T' on DZ O appeared ahead. The green came on again, and he jumped, to land spot-on the DZ, where the pathfinders had set up their lights in the correct place. A total of 2,090 men followed him. The majority of sticks landed on, or within a mile of, the DZ, some within two miles, and the remainder from five to 14 miles away. But it was a remarkable achievement.

On the 82nd's other DZs the drops were even more chaotic than on the 101st's. Again, pilots became disorientated by cloud, and lost their way weaving in flak. Some aircraft were hit and crashed. Many soldiers dropped into the flooded fields each side of the Merderet; some were drowned, or took hours to wade out on to dry ground. Others were killed or captured in small engagements, as they trudged towards the sound of fighting.

Lieutenant Colonel Edward Krause's 2nd Battalion of the 505th Parachute Infantry, was tasked with capturing St Mere-Eglise. An hour after landing his Battalion was only 108 strong at the RV. He set off for the town. Some 30 men of the regiment had dropped into the town, where an incendiary bomb had set fire to a house. The inhabitants were fighting the fire, while nearby German flak batteries engaged the C-47s flying overhead.

Some paratroopers dropped straight into the town square, to be killed by the Germans. Private Steele hung by his parachute from the church tower, and watched two fellow members of his mortar platoon land in the burning house, to be blown to pieces by the mortar bombs each member of the platoon carried.

When Krause arrived, all was quiet, most of the enemy amazingly having retired to their billets, leaving some dead Americans hanging in their parachute harness from nearby trees. Krause was able to clear the town easily, and, as more of his men reported in, was sufficiently strong to hold off counter-attacks.

General Ridgway took out his .45 pistol as he descended, to be ready to engage the enemy immediately on landing. He dropped it as he hit the ground. He took several frustrating minutes to find it, wondering if he, as divisional commander, would be the first man to lose his personal weapon. Joining up with his aide and a few others, he set up his command post in an orchard near St Mere-Eglise.

None of his radios arrived, and he could command only by touring on foot and in his jeep, after the gliders had landed. For 36 hours he was out of contact with VIIth Corps, and had absolutely no idea how the seaborne landings, or anything else outside his immediate vicinity, was progressing.

When D-Day ended, the 101st Airborne Division had accomplished the most important of its initial missions, although only 2,500 out of a jumping strength of 6,600 were operating within the divisional sector by last light. The way had been cleared for the advance inland of the seaborne forces. The northern flank of the corps front was secure. The southern flank was the main concern, where understrength units maintained a tenuous hold on some objectives, but were not strong enough to capture the bridges across the Douve.

The situation in the 82nd Airborne Division sector was more serious. Because of the scattered drop, the plan to gain immediate possession of both banks of the Merderet River could not be realised. Large numbers of the division were cut off west of the river.

Fortunately because of the efforts of the airborne divisions, the sea landings had been virtually unopposed, and the reinforcements so sorely needed by the 82nd and 101st were at hand.

On every possible invasion beach the Germans had constructed numerous obstacles, many mined, that were covered at high water To allow demolition teams to clear these dryshod, the landings on all beaches were timed for three hours before high water. Because of the tidal flow, high water on *Utah* was 40 minutes earlier than on *Sword*, at the eastern end of the Normandy lodgement area, The United States 4th Infantry Division was destined to be the first Allied formation to step ashore on the beaches of Normandy on 6 June 1944. At 04:30 (H minus two hours), detachments of the 4th and 24th Cavalry Squadrons landed on the Iles St Marcouf, to capture what was thought to be an observation post, or minefield control point. The main body of the cavalry detachment was preceded by four men, who, armed only with knives, swam ashore to mark the beaches. Both islands were unmanned, but heavily mined.

The coastal batteries on, and covering, Utah were silent. During the night they had been struck by heavy bombers of the Royal Air Force, and again, 40 minutes before H-Hour by Marauders of the Ninth US Air Force. The batteries' gun control radars were jammed, while the 14-inch gun battleship USS *Nevada*, the 15-inch gun monitor HMS *Erebus*, the cruisers USS *Tuscaloosa* and *Quincy*, and HMS *Hawkins*, *Black Prince* and *Enterprise*, and eight destroyers, bombarded these batteries, and coastal defences, starting at H minus 40 minutes.

Preceded by a massive salvo of rockets from LCTs (R), and DD swimming tanks, the assault craft carrying two battalions of the United States 4th Infantry Division touched down on *Utah* Beach almost exactly at H-Hour. The DD tanks were the only specialised armoured vehicles from the variety offered that the Americans decided to use. On *Utah*, they played an important part in suppressing the fire of the defenders as the American infantry waded the last hundred yards, and crossed the open beach.

The assault was in the wrong place. Thanks to the swamping of two control craft, and the difficulty of making out landmarks on the low coastline shrouded by smoke and dust from the bom-

bardment, the two leading battalions came ashore about a mile south-east of the intended beach.

This proved to be a blessing, instead of the disaster it might have been. Accompanying the first wave of infantry was the assistant divisional commander, Brigadier General Theodore Roosevelt Jnr, who had volunteered to co-ordinate the initial attack on the beach strongpoints until the arrival of the Regimental Commander, Colonel Van Fleet.

Perhaps he wished to emulate the exploits of his father Teddy Roosevelt, who some years before he became President of the United States, had led his Rough Riders at the Battle of San Jacinto Hill in the Spanish American War.

Whatever his motives, when he realised the landing was in the wrong place, he made a personal reconnaissance of the area behind the beach to find the exit causeways. On his return to the beach, he decided that landings would continue despite being in the wrong place, and proceeded to co-ordinate the attack on the nearest enemy positions . As luck would have it, this part of the coast was less heavily defended than further north, and the obstacle belt thinner. Brigadier General Roosevelt was awarded the Congressional Medal of Honour for his initiative and leadership.

Behind the leading waves of the division, came army engineer and naval demolition teams, to clear the mined obstacles on the beach, and blow gaps in the obstacle belt behind the beach. By mid-morning, the division started pushing inland across the causeways, and by 13:00 hours the leading troops of 4th Infantry Division had linked up with the men of the 101st Airborne, holding the landward end of the causeways.

The 4th Infantry Division's losses for D-Day were amazingly low. The first two regiments ashore had 12 dead and 106 wounded. The whole division took only 197 casualties in the whole of the first day, and these included 60 men missing at sea. By nightfall, force U , under command of Rear Admiral D P Moon USN, had landed over 20,000 troops, 1,700 vehicles,and 1,600 tons of stores on *Utah* Beach.

American howitzers shell German forces retreating near Carentan.

D-Day June 6th 1944
A TRIUMPH OF AIR POWER

D-Day 6th June 1944

by Frank Wootton PPGAvA

THE ROYAL AIR FORCE
BENEVOLENT FUND
50TH ANNIVERSARY
COMMEMORATIVE
LIMITED EDITION

SIGNED BY FAMOUS D-DAY AIRMEN

Frank Wootton's superb limited edition celebrates the RAF's contribution to D-Day and is individually counter-signed by five leading pilots operational on that day. They are **J E 'Johnnie' Johnson** DSO, DFC, the top-scoring allied fighter pilot in Europe; **Bill Reid** VC of 617 Squadron, the 'Dambusters'; **Roland Beamont** DSO, DFC, the famous post-war test pilot; 'Guinea Pig' club member and Spitfire pilot **Geoffrey Page** DSO, DFC; and Typhoon leader **'Pinkie' Stark** DFC, AFC.

The Certificate of Authentication, which accompanies each of the 850 prints, describes their experiences, and the role of the RAF, on D-Day.

FRANK WOOTTON PPGAvA

Frank Wootton was the official artist to the RAF in Normandy in 1944. His new painting shows 'Johnnie' Johnson leading Spitfires of his Canadian Wing over the beaches on D-Day.

J E 'Johnnie' Johnson

LIMITED EDITION

Each print in the D-Day Limited Edition is individually signed by Frank Wootton and five leading airmen. It is hand-numbered out of a total edition of 850. Measuring 24 x 30 inches, with an image area of 16½ x 24½ inches, the print is superbly reproduced on high-quality acid-free paper and is available luxuriously framed in a rubbed gilt, antique finish moulding, as shown above, or as an unframed, mounted print.

Send completed order form to:
Richard Lucraft Limited Editions, 62-63 Upper Street, London N1 0NY

THE OMAHA BEACHHEAD

UNITED STATES VTH CORPS

The V (US) Corps was allocated a stretch of the Normandy coastline between Port-en-Bessin in the East and the Vire Estuary in the West. To its left the 2nd British Army had been allocated the coastline in front of Bayeux and Caen. To its right the VII (US) Corps was to land on the Contentin Peninsula. In that part of the Normandy coastline allocated to V Corps there was an abundance of cliffs and reefs. Major-General Leonard T Gerow, V Corps Commander, selected a 7,000 yard cliffless interval between the cliffs to make his assault landing.

This five-mile stretch of shoreline was designated *Omaha* Beach. The beach sloped very gently below high water mark. With a tidal range of 18 feet expected at the time of the assault, low tide would expose a stretch of sand averaging about 300 yards in distance from low-water mark to high. The Germans had placed underwater obstacles on this tidal flat. At high water mark, the tidal flat ended in a bank of coarse shingle sloping up steeply to a height of some eight feet. On the eastern two-thirds of the beach, the shingle lay against a low sand embankment which was impassable to vehicles. On the western end of the beach there was a low seawall varying in height from four to 12 feet. Beyond the beach was an area about 200 yards wide of flat grass covered with sand from which rose a 150-ft bluff which dominated the whole beach area.

Omaha Beach lay in the 53-mile sector defended by the 716th Infantry Division, consisting of two infantry regiments, two or three artillery battalions and other small divisional units. It was estimated that defending troops in the *Omaha* Beach strongpoints amounted to perhaps a reinforced battalion, some 800 to 1000 troops. The division held three battalions within two hours of the beach as local reserves. Mobile reserves were some 20 miles inland. The nearest of these to *Omaha* Beach was the 352nd Infantry Division, an offensive division of good quality commanded by Lieutenant General Heinz Hellmich. It was at full strength with three infantry regiments with three battalions of 150mm artillery in support. Elements of this division would take perhaps eight hours to reach the beachhead.

Top
US infantry approach Omaha Beach in an LCVP (the American equivalent to the British LCA).

Left
Follow-up waves land on Omaha once the beach is secure.

The German plan was to stall, and if possible to defeat, the enemy landing on the beaches by a combination of firepower and obstacles. The reserves would arrive in time to finish off the enemy forces still struggling to gain a foothold.

The beach defences themselves consisted of a series of strongpoints each providing cleared fields of fire across the beaches.

Nearly all weapons, machine guns and artillery, were sited to provide lateral and flanking fire along the length of the beaches. In addition to all of this the Luftwaffe was expected to make a supreme effort on D-Day, making up to a total of 700 sorties.

The landings on *Omaha* Beach were preceded by intensive air and naval bombardment (see Preparatory Operations). H-hour was set at 0630. At first it seemed as if all would go according to plan. The landing craft came in under the covering fire from supporting naval guns, as well as from the tank and artillery pieces firing from LCTs.

It seemed that the enemy shore defences might have been neutralized but as the landing craft neared the beach they began to come under intense machine gun and artillery fire.

Survivors from some craft reported hearing a tattoo of bullets, on the ramps before they were lowered, followed by a hail of fire whipping up the sea just in front of the lowered ramps. Many men went over the sides and under the sea to escape the killing zone of the machine guns. Others were exhausted before they reached the shore where they faced 200 yards of open beach before reaching the cover of the seawall or shingle bank. In some of the initial assault companies casualties were as high as 70 per cent. One of the companies of the 2nd Ranger Battalion on the right of the assault lost 35 men from a total of 64 before it made it to the shelter of the seawall.

By 0700 the 116th Infantry battalion in the leading wave had lost all cohesion: 'E' company had veered off course a

mile to the east and lost contact, 'A' Company had been cut to pieces on the water's edge, 'F' Company was disorganized by heavy losses and the scattered sections of 'G' Company, which had suffered the least casualties, were preparing to move west along the beach to find their assigned sector.

Losses in equipment were also high during the first landings. The 397th anti-aircraft battalion lost 28 of its 36 machine guns whilst disembarking and infantry units experienced great difficulty in getting their heavy weapons ashore.

There was also a problem of morale. Behind the men of the initial assault wave, who were sheltering behind the seawall, many without officers or senior NCOs, the tide was drowning wounded men who had been cut down on the sands and was carrying bodies ashore just below the shingle.

Landing craft were still being hit and sunk further out at sea. Although these men were pinned down and desperately needed supporting fire, naval gunfire had virtually ceased when the troops reached the beach. The ships were under orders not to fire for fear of hitting American troops until fire control parties had established contact.

At 0800 hours, German soldiers looking down on the desperate plight of the assaulting troops probably felt that they had stopped the invasion at the water's edge. In fact at three or four places along the beach, American soldiers had left the cover of the seawall and had started to move out across the open space behind the beach to the bluffs beyond; they were helped in this move by the cover provided by the smoke from the burning grass. It took half-an-hour for the leading elements to reach the bluff top.

As Colonel George A Taylor, Commanding Officer of the 116th Infantry arrived on the beach at 0815, men were still suffering casualties from mortar and artillery fire. he uttered the memorable exhortation:

"Two kinds of people are staying on this beach, the dead and those who are going to die - now let's get the hell out of here".

Groups of men were collected regardless of which unit they belonged to, put in charge of the nearest NCO, and sent forward through the wire and minefields towards the bluff.

Naval gunfire support became more and more effective as the morning wore on. The few tanks that were landed also started to take on enemy strongpoints. As the assaulting troops slowly worked their way inland they encountered further resistance in the three villages of Vierville, St Laurent and Coleville.

At nightfall the German defenders were still putting up a stiff resistance in and around these three villages. The assault on *Omaha* had succeeded but the going had been much harder than expected. Stubborn enemy resistance had held the advance to a piece of ground no more than a mile-and-a-half deep in the Coleville area and considerably less than the west of St Laurent. US V Corps had suffered in the region of 3,000 killed, wounded or missing on D-Day.

The German resistance had been stiffened by reinforcements from the 352nd Division which had come forward from reserve positions and actually occupied many of the beach strongpoints already held by the 726th Regiment. This early use of reserves, although it made the initial landings more difficult, may have explained the lack of a properly coordinated German counter attack during the afternoon or evening of D-Day. also crucial to the survival of V Corps was the almost complete absence of the Luftwaffe.

It took until 11th June for V Corps to win sufficient ground to ensure the security of its beachhead. Although V Corps had enormous difficulty in developing its beachhead, the Allied operation achieved a good measure of success elsewhere.

In the Cotentin, the VII Corps landing from the sea had been a good deal easier and part of the 4th division was six miles inland.

To the east, the British Second Army landing had achieved an impressive early success and was in places holding ground as far as six miles inland. Quite clearly in the days after D-Day, the success of the VII Corps and Second British Army put pressure on the German defenders facing V Corps.

On 13th June V Corps received orders from Headquarters 1st Army which effectively marked the end of the *Omaha* beachhead operation. Starting from the most tenuous of footholds on D-Day, V Corps had driven inland with great difficulty 15-20 miles on a broad front.The crisis had been in the first 48 hours when the initial assault had met an unexpectedly strong enemy defence on the beach. The resilience of American soldiers and their ability to overcome chaos and lapses in leadership, led in the end to a notable victory.

Omaha Beach was the closest to failure of all the beach landings. In the final analysis, though, V Corps faced the crisis and won.

GOLD BEACH
BRITISH 50TH INFANTRY DIVISION

Gold Beach was on the extreme right of the British landing area, covering a 10-mile stretch of coastline between Port-en-Bessin and la Riviere. Part of it, from Port-en-Bessin to Arromanches-les-Bains, could not be used because of its rocky beaches and steep bluffs, so the landing was concentrated along five miles of open beach, divided into landing sectors codenamed Item, Jig and King.

Lieutenant-General Corfield Bucknall's XXX Corps was responsible for the landings, deploying two brigade groups of the 50th (Northumbrian) Division commanded by Major-General D A H Graham, 231 Brigade Group, comprising 2nd Battalion The Devonshire Regiment, 1st Battalion The Hampshire Regiment and 1st Battalion The Dorsetshire Regiment, was to come ashore in the central sector (Jig), with 69 Brigade Group, comprising 5th Battalion The East Yorkshire Regiment, 6th and 7th Battalion The Green Howards (Alexandra, Princess of Wale's Own Yorkshire Regiment), landing concurrently to the east (King).

No. 47 (Royal Marines) (RM) Commando was to follow 231 Brigade ashore. Their operations are described in the Chapter on Commandos.

Duplex-Drive (DD) tanks of the 4th/7th Royal Dragoon Guards were to provide close support during the landings, with ordinary armour of the Nottinghamshire (Sherwood Rangers) Yeomanry coming ashore as soon as possible to spearhead the drive towards Bayeux and the high ground to the east and west of the town.

The naval bombardment of shore positions ended abruptly at 0720 hours on 6th June, having concentrated against known enemy defences all along the British assault area for nearly two hours.

This disrupted the command and control of the German 716th Infantry Division, manning the beach defences, although it had less effect on those elements of the more experienced 352nd Infantry Division covering *Gold* Beach from bluffs inland.

Top
Number 48 (RM) Commando landing from LCIs (S) at St Aubin sur Mer.
Right
Follow-up waves landing on Gold Beach from Landing Craft Infantry (Large) (LCI(L)).
Overleaf
Landing Craft Tank (LCT) in the foreground and Landing Ships Tank (LST) off the coast of France on D-Day.

Even so, isolated pockets of defence still remained intact close to the shore, especially in the fortified seaside villages of le Hamel and la Riviere, while beach obstacles, ranging from minefields to mine-tipped steel posts at the low-water mark, remained. A 15-knot wind and rushing tide made it difficult for the infantry-carrying landing craft to navigate with complete accuracy.

As the naval bombardment continued, the decision was made not to launch the DD tanks off-shore, but to take them all the way in on board their landing craft. This would have the disadvantage of denying the infantry instantaneous support, but at least it could be virtually guaranteed that tanks would appear. It turned out to be a wise decision.

Nevertheless, the spearhead battalion of 231 Brigade, the 1st Hampshires, experienced some difficulties as they moved towards the shore-line at 0725 hours. A number of German gun positions, hidden from aerial reconnaissance or impossible to neutralise by naval bombardment, laid down heavy fire, particularly from the direction of le Hamel, while the wind and heavy surf forced the landing craft eastwards within Jig sector.

As the battalion landed, it suffered significant casualties that threatened to disrupt its cohesion. The commanding officer and most of his forward headquarters, including the artillery liaison officers, were hit and many of the battalion radios were destroyed, some by enemy fire and some in the actual process of landing.

For a time, the battalion was isolated, lacking the means to communicate with either ships or aircraft to bring down support fire. To cap it all, the second in command was killed, and OC C Company, Major Warren took command. Fortunately, the battalion was well trained and, immediate objectives were secured.

By 0800 hours, the second-wave battalion, the 2nd Devons, was coming ashore. An hour later, as the Hampshires fought for le Hamel ,a battle that was to engage them until late afternoon, the Devons pushed inland.

Meanwhile, to the east, the 1st Dorsets had landed across open beaches to consolidate the left flank of Jig sector, and armour had arrived. Flail tanks cleared passages through the minefields, while AVREs took out some of the concrete blockhouses that remained.

The assault in King sector, carried out by 69 Brigade Group, was equally successful. The spearhead battalions - 5th East Yorks and 6th Green Howards - landed at 0730 hours close to la Riviere, which was defended by machine-gun posts and a particularly effective 88 mm gun in an untouched bunker.

One of the supporting AVREs, risking destruction as it faced the bunker across open terrain, managed to manoeuvre itself on the blind side of the 88 mm and, with a single shot from its mortar, silenced the defenders. This allowed 5th East Yorks to leave the shelter of the seawall.

Meanwhile, to their right the 6th Green Howards had faced similar problems with a pillbox at Hable de Heurtot. However, the defenders in this case came up against Sergeant-Major Stanley Hollis who, virtually single-handed, captured the position, along with 25 rather confused German soldiers. Hollis was later awarded the Victoria Cross, the first of the campaign and the only one to be earned actually on the D-Day beaches.

By 0820 hours, as the reserve battalion - 7th Green Howards - came ashore, it was able to by-pass the fighting around and in la Riviere, pushing forward to take up positions on the Meuvaines Ridge, about a mile inland.

Although fighting was to continue at various locations until late afternoon on 6th June - notably to clear both le Hamel and la Riviere - *Gold* Beach was effectively secure by mid-morning, when the first of the Sherwood Rangers' tanks came ashore. This allowed General Graham to consolidate and begin to advance inland, leaving the beaches to be cleared of mines by flail tanks of the Westminster Dragoons and prepared for follow-up formations.

Three self-propelled artillery regiments landed with the tanks, ready to provide close support to the infantry, and beach groups of infantry and engineers began to sort out the inevitable chaos, setting up store areas and directing new units towards the cleared beach exits.

Meanwhile, 151 Brigade Group, comprising the 6th, 8th and 9th Battalions The Durham Light Infantry, landed between 1100 and 1130 hours. Despite sounds of heavy fighting from the direction of le Hamel and problems posed by a 'very rough and choppy sea', the landing was unopposed. Indeed, as one of the soldiers of the 8th DLI was heard to remark, '*It's a good thing there are no Germans about. We're so wet we couldn't even argue with them, let alone fight them!*'.

After consolidating, all three DLI battalions moved south to occupy the main road that ran between Bayeux and Caen. By then, the last of the assault formations, 56 Brigade Group, comprising 1st Battalion south Wales Borderers, 2nd Battalion The Gloucestershire Regiment and 2nd Battalion The Essex Regiment (an independent infantry brigade attached to 50th Division), had also come ashore, accompanied by the divisional commander and his staff.

As planned, the brigade moved off to the south-west, aiming to capture Bayeux. At first, German defenders melted away, but as they were bolstered in late afternoon by anti-tank units of the 352nd Infantry Division, opposition hardened.

At about 1600 hours, elements of 69 Brigade had to fight a tough battle to secure the villages of Villiers-le-Sec and Bazenville, and although this ended in a British victory, the experience may have persuaded commanders to exercise caution in case of sudden counter-attack. Certainly, there is evidence that 56 Brigade's advance slowed, finally halting on the outskirts of Bayeux. The town, D-Day objective, was not secured until early on 7th June.

But this should not detract from the overall success of the *Gold* Beach assault. By nightfall on 6th June some 24,970 men had come ashore between Arromanches-les-Bains and la Riviere and despite some hard fighting, had suffered less than 1000 casualties. Moreover, 69 Brigade, had managed to advance to a depth of eight miles, while 151 Brigade had severed the important Bayeux-Caen road.

On the beach itself, supplies and reinforcements, including the first units of 7th Armoured Division, were being landed. Most importantly, the 1st Hampshires, after clearing le Hamel, had spearheaded 231 Brigade to clear Arromanches, where Royal Engineer Port Construction units began to build the Mulberry Harbour. By D+12, the whole of XXX Corps was ashore, ready to expand a successful beachhead.

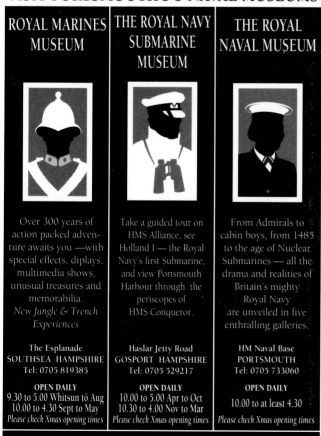

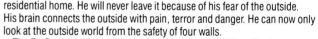

D-Day – the 50th Anniversary

Royal Doulton

6TH JUNE, 1944:

As the world's greatest seaborne invasion was launched from Portsmouth, Churchill's famous prediction four years earlier at last became a reality.

D-Day was truly a turning point in our history, and the beginning of the end of World War II. This powerful and symbolic tribute to one of the great leaders who inspired the allied forces to victory is released in celebration of the 50th Anniversary of the D-Day Landings.

Crafted in fine bone china by Royal Doulton, each plate is individually hand-numbered and accompanied by a correspondingly numbered Certificate of Authenticity.

To order *your* "We shall fight on the beaches..." plate - fully backed by The Bradford Exchange 365-day buy-back guarantee - simply complete the Priority Reservation Form and post it *today*.

"We shall fight on the beaches…"

A fine bone china collector's plate from Royal Doulton, available now at the issue price of £19.95 + p&p

THE BRADFORD EXCHANGE 365-DAY BUY-BACK GUARANTEE

If for any reason you are not completely satisfied, you may resell your plate to us at any time within one full year after you receive it. We will issue you a cheque for everything you have paid us, without question.
This guarantee is in addition to your statutory rights

PLEASE RESPOND WITHIN 14 DAYS*

Plate Diameter: 8 inches (20.5 c
With special hanging device for instant disp

NOTE: The quality of reproduction here may be inferior to that of the actual p

*Readers of this advertisement are asked to respond within 14 days. These plates are made by traditional methods - please allow up to 4-6 weeks for delivery. Offer applies UK only. The Bradford Exchange, Ltd, 1 Castle Yard, Richmond, Surrey TW10 6TF Reg. No. FC 14346 . Royal Doulton is a registered trademark.

THE BRADFORD EXCHANG

PF

SLAINTE MHÀTH!

Drambuie's military connection goes back 250 years to the brand's genesis, when the secret recipe for the elixir, made famous later as Drambuie, was handed to Captain MacKinnon by Bonnie Prince Charlie in return for saving his life after Culloden.

This special relationship has continued since, for it is widely acknowledged today that the origin of Drambuie's success world-wide can be traced back to the role played by the Scottish regiments since the outbreak of the Great War, when Drambuie had already received its first vote of approval in the regimental messes.

Since then, Scots stationed in every corner of the world have demanded the liqueur which reminded them of their homeland. It was thanks to this demand that the first seeds of Drambuie enjoyment were sown abroad. Soon, the demand for Drambuie gathered momentum with the result that today this fine liqueur is sold in over 160 countries and enjoyed by millions of people world-wide.

We would like to thank the Scots regiments for their vital contribution in introducing the finest of liqueurs to the world and wish them well on the occasion of the D-Day anniversary celebrations.

Slainte Mhàth!

JUNO BEACH
3RD CANADIAN INFANTRY DIVISION

Juno Beach, to the east of and contiguous with Gold, covered a six-mile stretch of coastline from la Riviere to the village of St Aubin-sur-Mer. Divided into three landing sectors, codenamed Love, Mike and Nan, it was to be assaulted by the 3rd Canadian Infantry Division, supported by the 2nd Canadian Armoured Brigade, part of Lieutenant-General John Crocker's British I Corps.

Top
Broached craft at St Aubin sur Mer. In the middle distance is an LCA. The beach markers on the right were set up by beach parties landing behind the leading waves.
Opposite
Ships of the Royal Canadian Navy approaching the French Coast on D-Day, 6th June 1944, showing Canadian soldiers preparing to go into battle.

The divisional commander, Major-General R F L Keller, decided to use two brigade groups to make simultaneous landings at 0735 hours.

On the right, 7 Canadian Infantry Brigade, comprising The Regina Rifle Regiment, Royal Winnipeg Rifles and 1st Battalion Canadian Scottish Regiment, was to come ashore around the small port of Courseulles (Mike and the edge of Nan).

They would be supported by DD tanks of the 6th Canadian Armoured

Regiment (The 1st Hussars). To their left, eight Canadian Infantry Brigade, comprising The Queen's Own Rifles of Canada, The North Shore Regiment and the French-Canadian Regiment de la Chaudiere was to land between Bernieres and St Aubin (Nan). They would be supported by DDs of the 10th Canadian Armoured Regiment (Fort Garry Horse

Some British units were to be involved in the assault - No. 48 (RM) Commando (whose actions are described in the Commando Chapter), C Squadron the Inns of Court Regiment, and Centaur tanks of the 2nd Royal Marines Armoured Support Regiment. The Beach Group included the 8th (Irish) Battalion, The King's (Liverpool) Regiment,

The landing area was not ideal. Offshore reefs obscured the approaches to much of Juno, making Love sector untenable, while the shoreline was dominated by rows of holiday villas and small villages.

German troops of the 716th Infantry Division had fortified many of the villages and laid extensive minefields; the beaches themselves contained the usual obstacles, particularly around the low-water mark. When it is added that on 6th June the seas were rough, it may easily be appreciated that the assault was always to be difficult.

In the event, the Canadians had to fight a hard battle to establish the beachhead. Assault engineers, ordered to clear lanes through the beach obstacles, were delayed by confusion offshore.

This, combined with an earlier decision to postpone the landing for ten minutes because of what appeared to be unmapped rocks (which turned out to be seaweed) on the approach route, meant that many of the obstacles were already covered by the tide when the landing craft came in. Battling through heavy surf and a racing tide, they inevitably suffered casualties.

Landing craft blew up as they nudged mines or came under fire from the shore - altogether on Juno Beach, 90 vessels were to be lost out of a total of 306 as the morning progressed - and infantry landed without the full benefit of armour support, sometimes straight into the teeth of enemy gun positions.

Even when they were ashore, many Canadian units found that they had to clear fortified villages and concrete blockhouses that had escaped the effects of the air and naval bombardments.

Spearheaded by the Regina Rifles and Royal Winnipeg Rifles, 7 Brigade Group landed at 0745 hours. Most of their supporting DDs arrived at the same time, having been launched into rough seas some 4,000 yards off-shore but six tanks were lost, leaving A Company of the Reginas to attack Courseulles on their own.

Predictably, they suffered heavy losses before clearing the built-up area. Similar problems affected the Winnipegs, landing to the west of Courseulles, who arrived without any tank support at all and were forced to advance using infantry weapons only; in the case of D Company, a difficult task as only 49 men had made it ashore from landing craft that had been badly disrupted by mines and obstacles.

Once ashore, the Winnipegs thrust inland to take the village of Banville - A Company had to fight hard to take out enemy positions at Ste Croix-sur-Mer - while the Reginas concentrated on subduing Courseulles and opening up beach exits.

The only unit of 7 Brigade to land virtually unopposed was the Canadian Scottish, one company of which accompanied the Winnipegs in the initial assault before capturing the Chateau Vaux. It was joined by the rest of the battalion a few hours later, enabling it and the Winnipegs to clear the villages of Vaux, Graye and Ste Croix.

Armoured cars belonging to the Inns of Court Regiment also landed in 7 Brigade area, suffering some losses to mines, while the 6th Field Company Royal Canadian Engineers was deployed to clear beach obstacles. By the end of the day, that particular company was to have suffered over 70 casualties out of a complement of 100 - one of the highest casualty rates anywhere on the British beaches.

Meanwhile, 8 Brigade had landed along the shore from Bernieres to St Aubin. Their assault had been delayed until 0755 hours, exacerbating the problems caused by the tide, which raced in to cover many of the beach obstacles before the landing craft arrived.

As a result, losses were heavy. In addition, the decision had been made not to launch the DD tanks of the 10th Armoured Regiment, leaving them in their landing craft to be

This Page
Assault craft en route for Normandy.
Opposite
D-Day off Juno Beach.
Inset
Canadian troops coming ashore on Juno Beach.

landed in the normal way. Given the losses in 7 Brigade area when DDs were ordered to 'swim' ashore, this was undoubtedly a sensible move, but it did mean that the vessels carrying the tanks had to wait until the infantry landing craft had gone in.

By then, the Queen's Own Rifles of Canada had managed to land, only to be forced to take shelter behind a seawall, under enemy fire. Les Wager of C Company described the moment of landing:

'The ramp dropped and we poured out in single file into waves up to our waists, running. Idiot orders were being shouted: "Off the beach! Off the beach! Get to the wall!" Relieved someone's tension, I suppose, but I don't know anybody who had to be told what to do on that beach'

In fact, the Queen's Own Rifles faced a tough task, landing without tank support directly in front of strongly fortified positions at Bernieres. They moved into the village without much delay, only to find it heavily defended. In house-to-house fighting, the regiment lost 143 men before being relieved by the arrival of DDs and AVREs.

One result of this was that when the follow-up battalion, the Regiment de la Chaudiere, arrived at Bernieres at 0930 hours, little had been done to clear the beach of obstacles.

Coming in on a rising tide, four landing craft were badly damaged by mines, the 'Chauds' at one point thought that they had lost most of their weapons. Some of the French-Canadians landed armed with nothing more than fighting knives, although in the event the crisis passed. By 1030 hours, Bernieres had been cleared and the Canadians were preparing to advance inland.

By comparison, the North Shore Regiment seemed to have a relatively easy time, coming ashore across a beach that was 'fairly quiet except for sniping'. However German opposition soon stiffened, particularly in St Aubin itself, which had to be taken house by house with AVRE support, delaying beach clearance.

The confusion on the beaches also affected the follow-up brigade, which was supposed to land at St Aubin and advance to seize the airfield at Carpiquet, to the west of Caen, before the end of the day. Meanwhile, 9 Canadian Infantry Brigade, comprising The Highland Light Infantry of Canada, The Stormont, Dundas and Glengarry Highlanders, and The North Nova Scotia Highlanders, had to be diverted to Bernieres at 1140 hours, but this did little to solve the problems.

By then, the landing area had been restricted in width by the tide, so that nearly everything from armour and artillery to reserve infantry and supplies was being forced into a bottleneck. Thus, although 9 Brigade landed without heavy losses, it could advance no further than the centre of Bernieres where, according to the Canadian Official History, it waited, 'complete with bicycles', for a way to be cleared.

It was not until early afternoon that the North Nova Scotias began their march inland, leaving it too late to reach Carpiquet that day.

By then, the Canadian beaches were secure - indeed, despite the chaos and losses, *Juno* was arguably the most successful landing area, even making contact with British troops from *Gold* Beach to the west before dusk.

During the day, 21,400 men came ashore in Mike and Nan sectors, losing 340 killed, 574 wounded and 47, taken prisoner. Some of the more distant objectives, such as Carpiquet, may not have been secured - and this was to cause problems in the future - but the Canadians could be justly proud of their achievements.

SWORD BEACH

3RD BRITISH INFANTRY DIVISION

The most easterly of the five D-Day beaches, codenamed *Sword*, covered a five-mile stretch of shore from St Aubin-sur-Mer to the coastal town of Ouistreham. Subdivided into sectors known as Oboe, Peter, Queen, and Roger, it was the objective of the 3rd British Infantry Division commanded by Major-General T G Rennie, part of Lieutenant-General J T Crocker's British I Corps. At first sight, the beaches seemed ideal, with level sand leading up to a small seawall along much of their length, but appearances were deceptive.

Rocks offshore acted as barriers off Oboe, Peter and part of Queen, forcing Rennie to concentrate assault formations along a three-mile frontage from Lion-sur-Mer on his right to Ouistreham on his left (part of Queen and whole of Roger.)

His orders were to establish a foothold, move inland to seize a number of known German strongpoints before advancing to take Caen, and to link up with elements of the British 6th Airborne Division along the Caen Canal

LCTs loaded with Shermans of the 13/18th Hussars, who landed with the assault brigade on Sword Beach, seen here before sailing for D-Day. A Sherman Firefly, equipped with a 17 pounder gun is in the nearest LCT.

Queen White Sector of Sword Beach on D-Day from the air.

and Orne River. In short, Rennie was to secure the left flank of the assault area.

Because of the restricted frontage, it was impossible to deploy more than a single brigade in the initial assault. Rennie chose 8 Infantry Brigade Group, comprising 1st Battalion The Suffolk Regiment, 2nd Battalion The East Yorkshire Regiment and 1st Battalion The South Lancashire Regiment (Prince of Wale's Volunteers). Spearheaded by DD (Amphibious) tanks of the 13th/18th Royal Hussars, AVREs of 5 Assault Regiment Royal Engineers, Flails of the Westminster Dragoons and Centaurs of the Royal Marine Armoured support Regiment, the infantry were to land at 0725 hours to the west of the hamlet of la Breche.

They were then to strike inland towards Hermanville-sur-Mer and probe east and west from the initial lodgement. Strongpoints codenamed 'Cod', 'Sole', 'Daimler', 'Morris, and 'Hillman' were to be taken, clearing the way for follow-up formations. Simultaneously elements of the 1st Special Service (Commando) Brigade under Brigadier Lord Lovat were to land. (The tasks and operations of 1st SS Brigade are described in the Commando Chapter). The remainder of 3rd Infantry Division would then land, consolidate the beachhead and advance towards Caen.

The naval and air bombardment of enemy positions, manned by elements of the 736th Grenadier Regiment, was still going on when, at 0615 hours, the first of the DD tanks

were launched some 5,000 yards off-shore. They were to land ahead of the infantry and, with other armoured units, clear paths through the beach obstacles.

As they ploughed through heavy seas, losing a total of 12 vehicles (out of 40) to a mixture of swamping and enemy fire, LCAs containing men of the 2nd East Yorks and 1st south Lancs approached the hostile shore.

The racing tide was already covering the mined obstacles at low-water mark, making the run-in extremely dangerous, and preliminary bombardments had not subdued every enemy position. Nevertheless, the initial landing went remarkably smoothly - the infantry had expected to suffer heavy casualties

just getting ashore, although by 0725 hours most were so sea-sick that they hardly seemed to care - and co-ordination between infantry and armour worked well.

Major A D Rouse of the 1st South Lancs described the scene: 'During the last 100 yards of the run-in everything seemed to happen at once. Out of the haze of smoke, the underwater obstacles loomed up ... and as we weaved in between iron rails and ramps and pickets with Teller mines on top like gigantic mushrooms we seemed to be groping through a grotesque petrified forest ... Mortar fire was coming down on the sands, an 88mm gun was firing along the line of the beach and there was continuous machine-gun and rifle fire'. Even so, casualties on the run-in were slight.

Once ashore, the assault troops cleared strongpoints overlooking the beach and then fanned out inland. This allowed the 1st Suffolks to land, closely followed by the commandos, who suffered about ten per cent casualties as German defenders recovered form the shock of invasion. No 41 (RM) Commando, together with men of the 1st South Lancs, advanced towards Lion, only to find it heavily defended; as some of the commandos by-passed the village to the south, others carried out a direct assault, clearing half of it as the day progressed.

The rest of the 1st South Lancs moved south towards Hermanville, securing it by 0900 hours. By then, No 4 Commando, with two troops of No 10 (Inter-Allied) Commando had advanced east towards Ouistreham, although they were delayed by the need to clear la Breche in company with men of the 2nd East Yorks.

That particular firefight continued until 100 hours, after which the 2nd East Yorks pushed forward into the southern outskirts of Ouistreham (the town was, symbolically, liberated later that morning by Free French commandos).

This enabled the 1st Suffolks to advance through Colleville-sur Orne towards the 'Hillman' strongpoint. Protected by mines, barbed wire and machine guns, ' Hillman' proved to be a tough nut to crack. Corporal Rayson of A Company of the Suffolks later recalled one of the assaults: *'We crawled through a field of barley and waited till the Engineers lifted some mines and taped a track through. Another party got rid of the wire with Bangalore torpedoes. Then we went in. The first two, a corporal and a private, were killed as soon as they got through the gap ... We all got down and he kept us down...'* The stongpoint was not completely cleared until early the next morning.

Elements of 3rd Infantry Division's follow-up brigade group began to land just after 0900 hours on 6th June. Comprising the 2nd Battalion Royal Warwickshire Regiment, 1st Battalion Royal Norfolk Regiment and 2nd Battalion The King's Shropshire Light Infantry, 185 Brigade Group had the ambitious task of taking Caen.

Delayed by the late arrival of their supporting tanks - the Shermans of The Staffordshire Yeomanry were caught up in the chaos on the beaches and did not link up with the infantry until early afternoon - 185 Brigade moved off alone at noon. The 2nd Warwicks captured Blainville-sur-Orne, to the south-west of the Orne bridges, while the 1st Norfolks and 2nd KSLI moved to left and right of the 1st Suffolks, in front of 'Hillman'.

The Norfolks particularly suffered significant casualties as they came within range of the strongpoint, although it was the KSLI who encountered the heaviest enemy opposition.

Main Picture
The back of Sword Beach, with Commandos moving inland through engineers clearing mines.
Top Right
Beach Group setting up after landing.
Top Left
Troops on a British Beach on D-Day, digging in and attending to casualties. Probably a Beach Group or Beach Party. An AVRE with Petard mortar is on the right.

107

By 1600 hours, they had advanced as far as the Bieville-Periers ridge, where they were counter-attacked by elements of 21st Panzer Division, probing north along the gap between Sword and Juno Beaches. By then, the Staffordshire Yeomanry had caught up and they, together with anti-tank guns belonging to the KSLI and the 20th Anti-Tank Regiment Royal Artillery, managed to blunt the attack, destroying a total of 13 panzers. Air support was called down and the enemy withdrew, although 185 Brigade could only advance to within three miles of Caen by the end of the day. Another counter-attack by 21st Panzer at 1900 hours, spearheaded by 50 tanks, almost reached the sea at Lion, but was stopped just short of its objective.

By then, the whole of 3rd Infantry Division was ashore, having landed its reserve brigade group as the day progressed. Comprising the 2nd Battalion Lincolnshire Regiment, 1st Battalion The King's Own Scottish Borderers and 2nd Battalion Royal Ulster Rifles, supported by The 1st East Riding yeomanry, 9 Brigade Group initially moved south-west towards its objective of Carpiquet airfield, where it was to link up with Canadians from *Juno* Beach.

As German opposition hardened, however, Rennie diverted the brigade to the south-east to reinforce the line of the Orne River. This meant that any chance of taking Caen on 6th June was effectively lost - something that was to have far-reaching consequences in the coming weeks - but more immediately it also meant that the gap between *Sword* and *Juno* could not be closed. Thus, although the assault on *Sword* Beach was undoubtedly a success - 3rd Infantry Division put 28,845 men ashore on 6th June and suffered less than 1,000 casualties, killed and wounded - some of the D-Day objectives had not been seized and the left flank of the Allied assault area was to remain on the defensive for some days.

As troops and supplies poured ashore over the next few days, they were involved in an unseen battle to ensure that they consolidated their foothold before German Panzer reserves, called in from as far away as Toulouse, arrived in Normandy. The seaborne landing may have gone well, but the subsequent breakout was going to be a hard-fought engagement.

Beachmasters's HQ in Normandy

THE COMMANDOS

'They performed whatsoever the King commanded'
Samuel II

Inscription on the Commando memorial in Westminster Abbey

The commandos were originally raised in the aftermath of Dunkirk and the fall of France, to raid and harass the enemy against the day when the British Army would return to France in strength. By the time that day arrived, on 6th June 1944, as well as mounting raids on the continent of Europe, commandos had fought in most theatres of war, often as part of the main battle. Increasingly they were given tasks on the flanks, or ahead of the main force; counting on their training and elan to overcome difficulties that might have daunted more conventional units. The roles given to the commandos for the invasion of Normandy were no exception.

Two Special Service (SS) Brigades of commandos were available for the operation. These Brigades, re-named commando Brigades in November 1944, to avoid the SS title consisted of Army and Royal Marines (RM) Commandos as follows:

1ST SS BRIGADE
Brigadier the Lord Lovat

3 COMMANDO	4 COMMANDO	6 COMMANDO	45 (RM) COMMANDO
Lt Col P Young	Lt Col R W P Dawson	Lt Col D Mills Robert	Lt Col N C Ries

4TH SS BRIGADE
Brigadier B W Leicester

41 (RM) COMMANDO	46 (RM) COMMANDO	47 (RM) COMMANDO	48 (RM) COMMANDO
Lt Col T M Gray	Lt Col C R Hardy	Lt Col C F Phillips	Lt Col J L Moulton

In 1944, a commando consisted of a headquarters; five rifle troops, each about 60 strong; and a support troop consisting of a 3-inch mortar platoon of four mortars, a Vickers medium machine gun platoon with four guns, and an assault engineer platoon. Total fighting strength was around 450 all ranks.

Lovat's 1st SS Brigade was to operate east of the River Orne under command of the British 6th Airborne Division. The Brigade was to land on the left of Sword Beach, behind the leading infantry of the British 3rd Infantry Division. Number 4 commando was to land first and was tasked to destroy a battery and garrison in Ouistreham.

Men of Number 45(RM) Commando in their transit camp before embarking for Normandy. Many commandos landed with bicycles to speed up their progress inland. These, and the heavy loads each man carried, were in many cases to impede the swift disembarkation in the the far from ideal conditions on D-Day.

111

The Commando was reinforced by two French troops of Number 10 Inter allied (IA) Commando under Captain Kieffer. The remainder of 1st SS Brigade were to land some 20 minutes later, and march with all speed to the bridge over the Caen Canal at Benouville, which 6th Airborne Division was to have seized the night before. On completion of its task in Ouistreham, Number 4 Commando was to rejoin the Brigade east of the Orne.

The commandos of 4th SS Brigade all had independent tasks on D-Day. Number 41 (RM) Commando landing on Sword Beach was ordered to destroy coastal defences in the area of Lion-sur-Mer, and advance west to link up with 48 (RM) Commando advancing east from Juno Beach, in the village of Petit Enfer. Number 48 (RM) Commando having landed at St Aubin, had first to destroy coastal defences at Langrune. Number 47 (RM) Commando was to land on Gold Beach, under command of the British 50th Infantry Division, and passing through the leading troops of the Division, capture Port-en Bessin, the junction point of the British and American sectors of the beachhead. The port was also earmarked as one of the terminals for the pipeline under the ocean, PLUTO, through which fuel would be pumped direct from England. Its early capture was vital. Number 46 (RM) Commando was to remain afloat on D-Day ready to assault two coastal batteries east of the Orne at Houlgate and Benerville, should these start to threaten the landing beaches.

The Medical Officer (MO) of Number 4 Commando, who had fought in France in 1940 and Madagascar, described the run-in to Sword Beach in LCAs:

'We were rolling heavily in a big south-westerly swell which broke continually over us, drenching and chilling us to the marrow. My hands grew numb and dead, and my teeth were chattering with cold and fright. We passed round the rum, and those who were not too seasick took a good swig. The sea was well dotted with bags of vomit, and I could see the boys on the LCIs rushing to the rail.'

Like others landing after the initial waves, 4 Commando had to pass through a line of dead and wounded on the water-line. They could not stop, having to press on to their objective. The MO of Number 4 Commando;

'I noticed how fast the tide was rising, and the wounded men began to shout and scream as they saw they must soon drown.'

An officer of 45 (RM) Commando saw:

'A number of battle-dressed bodies, all face down, gently floating on the tide-line surrounded by a pinkish tinge. The sound of the adjutant's hunting horn made me gather my wits, impressing on me the need to make for the RV.'

Landing in second, third, or later waves could sometimes be more hazardous than arriving in the first. The landing craft, in which many from both SS Brigades landed, were especially vulnerable. These wooden-hulled craft, adapted from coastal forces boats, with unarmoured high octane petrol tanks in the bows, and originally designed for raids, took heavy casualties landing on such a heavily-defended shore. Private Holmes, back in Number 3 Commando, after recovering from being wounded in Italy:

'D-Day was to be my eighth landing with Number 3 Commando, but I was most unhappy about it for it was to be my first in daylight and the first time we were not to be first in. We were due to land after the hornet's nest had been disturbed.'

His craft was holed on the run-in, and he was badly wounded. He was one of the few to be rescued.

By about 11:00 hrs, Number 4 Commando had succeeded in capturing the coastal battery, but suffered many casualties, including Lieutenant Colonel Dawson, who was wounded twice. They reorganised, withdrew from Ouistreham, and set off to rejoin their brigade, which, led by Number 6 Commando, was already making for Benouville. Although 6 Commando tried to by-pass or infiltrate enemy positions, they had to overcome a number of strongpoints, and a gun battery to allow the remainder of the brigade to follow.

They covered the six-and-a-half miles in three-and-a-half hours, a remarkable achievement for lightly-equipped troops with no artillery support. Lord Lovat, his piper and Numbers 3 and 45 (RM) Commandos arrived after Number 6 Commando at 14:00 hrs. The bridge at Benouville was still under small arms fire from pockets of enemy overlooking it, which caused several casualties among the commandos as they crossed, including Lieutenant Colonel Ries, the commanding officer of 45 (RM) Commando. By nightfall, 1st SS Brigade had taken up defensive positions on the left flank of 6th Airborne Division, along the ridge running through Amfreville-Le Plein-Hauger, which gave observation over the landing beaches. Number 45 (RM) Commando was ordered to push up the coast to Franceville Plage to prevent enemy access from the north.

For the next four days the enemy mounted a series of attacks against the Brigade's positions on the ridge. All were repulsed with considerable enemy casualties. Meanwhile Number 45 (RM) Commando had dug in some 500 yards short of Franceville Plage, forming a tight defended area. On the following day two heavy German counter-attacks were beaten off. But by D+3, the build up of enemy troops around the Commando and the increasing shelling and mortar fire were such that the Commando was ordered to fight its way back into the Amfreville area. After a three-hour battle, this was achieved.

On 10th June, the enemy launched a very heavy attack against the brigade. The main effort directed against Number 6 Commando, but eventually the attack died down without any loss of the brigade's vital ground. Later that day, the attack was switched to Number 4 Commando's position on the left of the brigade. After fierce fighting the Germans were finally beaten off. During four days of intense fighting the brigade had suffered heavy casualties. Many Germans were killed and taken prisoner. But the Amfreville ridge had been held.

The commandos of 4th SS Brigade had, if anything, a rougher landing than 1st SS Brigade. Number 41 (RM) Commando was landed some 300 yards west of their intended beach, taking heavy casualties. Finding the strongpoint at Lion-sur-Mer deserted, the Commando advanced to attack a strongly held chateau beyond the village, which was later reinforced by German tanks and infantry; remnants of 21st

Headquarters 1st SS Brigade landing on Sword Beach. Brigadier Lord Lovat is the lone figure on the right of the troops wading ashore.

Panzer Division's attempted counter-attack to the coast. Without supporting fire, because the two Forward Observation Officers (FOO), had been killed, and lacking armoured support, the Commando could only neutralise the strongpoint. It was captured the next day by 2nd Battalion the Lincolnshire Regiment, of 3rd Infantry Division.

Number 48 (RM) Commando, in LCI's (S), suffered heavy casualties on landing. They would have been heavier had not the commanding officer previously trained his commando to fire 2-inch mortar smoke from the bows of their craft during the run in to the beach. Although the resulting smoke-screen shielded the craft from direct enemy fire, beach obstacles and shrapnel holed the wooden hulls, killing and wounding the troops and crews. Most craft did not beach square on to the water line, and the heavily-laden troops were very exposed as they scrambled down the steep bow gangways, which pitched and lurched in the swell, and waded through the waist-deep water. Some men were unceremoniously thrown off head first into the sea. Some were swept off by the swift current and drowned while trying to swim ashore from broached craft.

Although the commanding officer was wounded by fragments from a mortar bomb, he directed his men to the assembly area, to find that he had only 50 per cent of his Commando, before even beginning his allotted task. Moving through St Aubin, where the Canadians were fighting to over-come a major strongpoint, the Commando advanced to Langrune, two miles east of St Aubin. Here the Germans had established a strongpoint consisting of a block of old houses, and streets full of wire and mines. Despite the lack of sup-porting fire, consisting of the one surviving 3-inch mortar and a handful of tanks, one of which succeeded in throwing a track and blocking the road, the commando made several attempts to overcome the strongpoint.

Eventually Brigadier Leicester, expecting a German counter attack ordered Moulton to halt and take up defensive posi-tions. The next day, 48 (RM) Commando captured Langrune. The first two days had cost the Commando 217 all ranks dead, wounded and missing.

In capturing Port-en-Bessin, Number 47 (RM) Commando had one of the more daunting tasks, involving a ten-mile march beyond the forward line of friendly troops. The Commando embarked in 14 LCAs from two LSIs, and the run-in was uneventful until about 2,000 yards form the beach. Major Donnell, then the second-in-command:

'It became obvious that Jig Green beach was deserted except for four support tanks under heavy fire. At about this time a 75mm battery on the high ground above Le Hamel opened accurate fire on the LCAs.
The CO ordered a turn to port and all craft in some disorder, started running parallel to the beach. Each craft picked its own landing place. Very few had had a dry landing; most grounding offshore, in some cases

on obstacles in water so deep that the only way ashore was to dump equipment and swim. One craft ran into a mine and had its bows blown off. Of the 14 craft, only two returned to the LSIs. The landing was a shambles. The commando was spread over a frontage of some 1,500 yards. As planned the commando moved west, towards the RV, the church in Le Hamel. It soon became obvious that Le Hamel was in enemy hands, and 231 Brigade was heavily involved in clearing the town.'

Donnell made contact with the commander of 231 Brigade who suggested they swing south to avoid Le Hamel, before returning to the original route. Donnell:

'The CO, four officers and 73 other ranks were missing, practically all the bangalores and 3-inch mortars had been sunk. X and B Troops were reasonably dry and equipped, A Troop were complete, but had lost most of their weapons, Q and Y Troop had each lost a craft-load. There was only one Vickers and one 3-inch mortar out of four of each, and the latter was without a sight. Commando HQ was almost complete, but all the wireless sets were doubtful starters.'

The commando set off under the second-in-command. As they were moving round Le Hamel, the CO appeared riding on an ammunition sled behind a self-propelled gun. That night after by-passing or overcoming pockets of enemy, the Commando established a firm base on point 72, part of the high ground about two miles south of Port-en-Bessin. Many of the Commando were now armed with German weapons, for which there was no shortage of ammunition.

The next day, the Commando attempted to contact the American artillery whose support figured so prominently in the plan for the capture of the port; to no avail. Eventually communication was established with 231 Brigade of 50th Infantry Division, and ships offshore, including HMS Emerald. The attack started at 16:00 hrs, supported by naval and air bombardment, smoke from one of 231 Brigade's field batteries, and the one Vickers and the mortar without a sight. The fighting in the town was confused and bitter. Having secured one of the two features dominating the town, the other was

Left
Commandos and parachute soldiers in Normandy.
Below
Lieutenant Colonel J.L.Moulton, the commanding officer of 48(RM)
Commando in Langrune, watching a Sherman tank supporting his
commando.

captured at the second attempt by about midnight. The troop commander, Captain Cousins, having found a route through the wire, was killed leading the attack. The next day the commando was relieved; of the 431 who had embarked in the LCAs on D-Day, 276 remained. General Montgomery visited them to congratulate them.

Number 46 (RM) Commando, were not required to deal with the batteries at Houlgate and Benerville, and were instead ordered to land on Juno Beach on the morning of D+1 to capture the strong point at Petit Enfer. This task was accomplished by that evening. By this time Number 41 (RM) Commando had moved into the area from Lion-sur-Mer, and the two commandos, joined subsequently by 48 (RM) Commando, surrounded the radar station at Douvres, which was heavily wired and mined, with subterranean defences which were reported to have taken three years to build.

On 11th June Number 46 (RM) Commando was placed under command of the Canadian 3rd Infantry Division, and

117

given the task of clearing the Mue valley from the village of Barbiere up to the Caen-Bayeux road. The final phase of the attack involved taking the villages of Le Hamel and Rots. Here the Commando fought troops of the 12th SS (Hitler Jugend) Panzer Division, considerably more formidable than the majority of the enemy encountered in the coast defences.

Eventually, after a very tough battle, with tank support, the Commando captured both villages. The following day the divisional commander withdrew the commando, as operations on the flanks had made only limited gains. 122 German dead were found when the two villages were subsequently reoccupied by the Canadians. 46 (RM) Commando lost 20 killed, nine wounded and 31 missing.

On 12th June, Brigadier Leicester was ordered to take Numbers 47 and 48 (RM) Commandos across the Orne and occupy defensive positions in the Hauger and Sallenelles area, on the left of 1st SS Brigade. Number 46 (RM) Commando followed on completion of their battle in the Mue Valley. Number 41 (RM) Commando continued to mask the radar station at Douvres, until they were given sufficient support to capture it on 21st June. Then they joined 4th SS Brigade across the Orne. The Commandos of both brigades remained under the command of 6th Airborne Division on the left flank of the British sector, subsequently taking part in the breakout in August 1944, and the advance to the River Seine.

Commandos of the 1st SS Brigade moving inland. Weighed down with bergen rucksacks and ammunition, some were carrying in excess of 100Ibs.

118

THE BATTLE OF NORMANDY - D-DAY'S AFTERMATH

The invading forces were ashore on a frontage of 25 miles and an average depth of five. The first act of the great drama had closed. Inhibited by Allied domination of the air and by the powerful effect of ship-to-shore naval gunnery the German armour , on whose effectiveness in rapid counter-attack the whole issue turned , had failed to drive the Allies into the sea.

But the outcome was still uncertain. The only Panzer division in 21 Army Group's area immediately to hand on D-Day had been 21st Panzer but others were attempting to 'march to the sound of the guns'.

British infantry and armour along the main road to Vassey, 4 August 1944.

On 7th June, 12th SS Panzer Division attacked in the Canadian sector, and on 8th June Panzer Lehr Division arrived to counter-attack XXX Corps near Tilly-sur-Seulles. Five days later 2nd Panzer Division joined the fight, blocking the way south towards Villers-Bocage. The delay in the arrival, even by hours or a day of these divisions , badly mauled by air attack, meant that they faced ever greater strength. In the event their attacks were unsuccessful; the various elements of the Allied

invasion forces joined hands, and by 9th June a continuous front had been formed. A slow and painful expansion of the beachhead followed.

Difficult though movement was for the Germans, they managed to bring enough troops to the front to stop any rapid or ambitious Allied attempts forward, and their tactical skill was still formidable. The Norman countryside (except round Caen) largely consists of close bocage country of small fields and orchards, high, thick, hedges and sunken lanes. The mobility of armoured formations was everywhere checked and their prime weapon, the tank gun, could often only engage at a range limited by the next bank. Such country consumed troops in both attack and defence, offering few alternatives but to push from hedge to hedge, fighting for each as an infantry battle, supported by the close-range fire of tanks, themselves laboriously lumbering along the same trail. It was country in which the intimate co-operation of tanks and infantry, preferably organised and trained together, was the key to victory. In such country the huge Allied superiority in mechanised vehicles was often nullified, while German near-equivalence in infantry made its mark. German armour had been unable to intervene in force at the time of air and seaborne landings when the assaulting troops were most vulnerable. It could now only support local counter-attacks or act defensively in protracted blocking operations, but in this it was highly effective, the Panther and Tiger tanks doing particularly deadly work. German mortars and Nebelwerfer were

as menacing as ever. Expansion of the Normandy beachhead consisted of a huge patchwork of tactical engagements at very close quarters rather than a grand manoeuvre. But throughout June the beachhead expanded, and within it the Allied troop totals, remorselessly increased.

General Bernard Law Montgomery, commanding all land forces, was reasonably content with the progress of operations in the early days. He had not taken Caen, I Corps original objective, which the Germans were defending with tenacity. But Montgomery reckoned success not in ground gained but in terms of what was happening to the enemy's body and mind; and this was satisfying to him. The German Army was being worn down and deprived of opportunity or hope. Montgomery's concept was clear and consistent for the next phase of operations. "My general policy", he declared in a personal signal to the CIGS on 10th June, "is to pull the enemy on to 2nd Army so as to make it easier for 1st (US) Army to expand and extend quicker." On 18th June he wrote to his army commanders, "The enemy mobile reserves are becoming exhausted."

By that day the 1st US Army was half-way up the Cotentin peninsula and by 27th June its VII Corps had taken Cherbourg, the first port to supply the Allied forces, apart from the battered Mulberry Harbour. On 3rd July the US VIII Corps attacked south towards Coutances and St Lo, joined next day, 4th July by VII Corps. The battle of

Normandy was now a battle of attrition; of wearing down an out-numbered enemy with bombardment and with attacks by numerically-superior forces until their line broke.

They key to the security of the Allied beachhead was Caen, where the Germans held out. Montgomery's design was to envelop it from west and south. His increasing pressure in the east of the beachhead was intended to secure it against any attack from that direction: but was also, and principally, inspired by his intention to break out from the western sector, with American forces swinging south and eastwards through Mortain to Alencon and Le Mans, and detaching a corps to drive into Brittany. Thus a concentration of German Panzer divisions and local counter-attacks against General Dempsey's Second Army, in the eastern sector, was highly satisfactory to Montgomery, provided that Dempsey's front held.

This policy required unremitting activity on the Second Army Front, the country in the American Western sector being particularly difficult for an attacker. "In order to help the western sector I am going to set things alight on my eastern flank, beginning tomorrow," Montgomery wrote on 7th July. But he added, "We cannot be 100 per cent happy on the eastern flank until we have got Caen." A major Second Army attack was mounted on 8th July, with I Corps, consisting of 3rd and 59th (British) and 3rd (Canadian) Divisions, and next day Montgomery was able to signal: 'leading troops ... pushing on tonight towards centre of city.' The city of Caen itself had been pulverised by Allied bombing in support of this attack, bombing which caused heavy civilian casualties. West of Caen Montgomery ordered Second Army to continue its attacks southward to pin the German reserves, and to push to the general line Thury Harcourt - Mont Pincon - Le Beny Bocage; operation CHARNWOOD.

On the German side the daily increasing strength of the Allies, the unremitting air bombardment, and the pressure around Caen were causing despair. Field Marshals von Rundstedt and Rommel, respectively Commander-in-Chief West and Commander-in-Chief Army Group B, had tried in vain to convince Hitler on 29th June that the front could not be held, and that Hitler's order to 'stand fast' was condemning the troops to inevitable destruction. Von Rundstedt was immediately replaced by Field Marshal Von Kluge, while General Geyr Von Schweppenburg, Commander of 'Panzer Group West', most of the armoured troops opposing 21 Army Group, was also removed. Rommel was by now convinced that defeat was inevitable.

The 13 British divisions of 21 Army Group were now concentrated in the bridgehead; six weeks had gone by; and Montgomery decided on a major operation, to, in his own words, "loose a Corps of three armoured divisions into the open country about the Caen-Falaise road." Such an operation could not fail to attract such German reserves as were not already opposite the eastern sector of the beachhead, and was thus consistent with Montgomery's strategy. He thought, however, that more dramatic opportunities might conceivably present themselves.

The German positions east of Caen were sited in considerable depth, Rommel himself, certain that this would be the scene of the next major Allied attack, had visited the sector almost daily, ordering the deployments and establishing the principles of the defence: although both Panzer and infantry divisions were gravely depleted the Germans were still strong in anti-tank guns. Between the suburbs of Caen and the Bois de Bavent, to the east, is a level plateau of farmland dotted with coppices and small villages, and constituting something

The ruins of Caen, July 1944.

of a funnel. This was the ground on which Montgomery ordered Dempsey to commit his 'Corps of three armoured divisions' , VIII Corps, whose attack was to be a thrust between two flanking corps , 1 Corps on its left, with 3rd Division taking protective positions on the eastern flank, and II (Canadian) Corps on its right, with two divisions, extending the lodgement in Caen itself.

VIII Corps, consisting of the Guards, 7th and 11th Armoured Division, was to be driven south into the area of Vimont, St Aignan de Cramesnil, Verrieres, astride the Caen-Falaise road. Such force, poised for further advance, would, it was hoped bring upon itself all available German armour, and produce that 'writing down' of German strength which Montgomery had urged Dempsey to achieve. This was Operation GOODWOOD.

During the night of 17th July the three armoured divisions of VIII Corps moved eastwards behind the front towards the Orne bridges, and during the early hours of the morning the leading echelons began filing across those bridges, moved by taped routes through the minefields, and formed up ready for the southern attack. Meanwhile, in the pale morning light, the greatest aircraft concentration of its kind yet known, over 1,000 heavy and medium bombers supporting the tactical offensive, was directed on the target areas east of Caen over which the army was to advance. As the aircraft returned home, warships took up the bombardment, succeeded by further waves of aircrafts which continued the work for two hours after the forward movement began.

At 07:45 hours supported by a barrage of 200 guns, 11th Armoured Division began moving south. Opposing them were infantry of 16th German Air Force Division; but within reach were 1st SS and 21st Panzer Divisions albeit with a combined strength, by then, of no more than 100 tanks including, however, a number of Tigers. The defences, to a depth of eight miles, were based on the numerous villages and farms between Troarn in the east and the outskirts of Caen, and between Cuverville, in the north, and the Bourguebus Ridge. Within this area every cluster of buildings, every edge of wood and coppice, every hedgerow or reverse slope held anti-tank guns with infantry and machine-gun positions deployed to protect them. The country was open, but the front was narrow, little more than three miles, widening to no more than six.

The effect of the air bombardment was considerable. The defenders of the forward German defences were destroyed or dazed and the initial advance went well, with the tanks of 11th Armoured Division swinging down to and across the railway which ran south-east from Caen, bypassing strong points for later attention. By mid-morning, however they were held up, with considerable casualties, north of Bourguebus. The Guards Armoured Division, following them with the intention of swinging left and reaching Vimont, instead found itself enmeshed among the unsuppressed anti-tank guns and defenders of Cagny and Emieville. Meanwhile 7th Armoured Division, in rear, directed to come in on the left of 11th, was so held up by the appalling congestion that it could not reach the battle at all in any strength. To cram three armoured divi-

124

sions, flanked by infantry divisions with their own support echelons into the restricted area east of Caen was to ensure chaos unless the advance went swiftly. It did not. The German line was unbroken. Six miles were won but there was no question of 'a Corps of three armoured divisions in the open country about the Caen-Falaise road'. German tank losses had been high, beside 9th and 10th SS Panzer recently arrived from Russia, 12th SS Panzer and 116th Panzer Divisions from the eastern sector, and elements of 2nd Panzer from the centre of the Normandy front had moved to the scene of action and had suffered, but German strength had certainly not been 'written down' sufficiently to make break-out a formality. By 20th July Dempsey accepted that no more would be won in the area of Caen. GOODWOOD was over.

The operation had been successful in keeping the defenders' eyes and strength in the east - Montgomery's principal aim. He had undoubtedly envisaged the possibility, no more, of a victory which would have, in his words, 'destroyed all possible enemy troops in the general area Caen-Mezidon-Falaise, Evrecy, a victory which would have so stretched the German defences as to make break-out almost inevitable. It didn't happen.

Nevertheless Montgomery, always resilient, immediately resolved to turn this half-success to better effect elsewhere on 21 Army Group front. GOODWOOD had drawn most of the German armour facing the British to the east of the Orne, and in the centre there appeared to be little major opposition. Montgomery now ordered Dempsey to shift his weight from his left to his right foot; to move the whole of VIII Corps from the area of Caen to the area of Caumont; and to put in

as strong an attack as he could on 30th July, southwards, in the centre of the Allied front.

In the United States 1st Army sector, in western Normandy, VII Corps had reached positions commanding the St Lo, Periers road, and taken St Lo, by 20th July, the day GOODWOOD ended. On 25th the Americans attacked south, from the ground west of St Lo. This was Operation COBRA. Attacking on a narrow front, preceded by a massive air bombardment, the attackers reached Avranches on 30th July. German strength had been so eroded by now that the defenders could no longer prevent American moves to break in or outflank and the front was, for them, now dangerously extended.

Meanwhile, in 21 Army Group's sector, Second Army's attack south from Caumont had first to win a lodgement on the high wooded feature known as Mont Pincon, running from the banks of the Orne at Thury Harcourt to St Martin des Besaces and the Foret L'Eveque. On the left XXX Corps was to attack with 43rd and 50th Division towards the western end of Mont Pincon, while on the right VIII Corps was to go for some high ground with 15th Division. 11th Armoured Division was to take St Martin des Besaces while Guards and 7th Armoured Divisions were in reserve.

This was Operation BLUECOAT, which lasted until 6th August. Progress was slow but relentless, straining the whole fabric of German defence, just as the Americans had now fatally strained it in Operation COBRA in the west. Kluge, taking a very personal control of the battle, was near despair. He moved 21st Panzer Division from east to west on the first day, to counter-attack in the area won by 15th Division and to hold the high ground of St Martin des Besaces, On the British right 11th Armoured Division outflanked the enemy in the Foret l'Eveque and reached the Souleuvre River, while on 11th Division's left the Guards Armoured Division was directed on Le Tourneur.

On 1st August 11th Armoured Division fought its way into Le Beny-Bocage. The Caumont sector of the front was now clearly critical for the Germans and Kluge moved II Panzer

Above
Infantry and armour moving through Gace, between Argentan and Laigli 21st August, 1944.
Right
Beny Bocage, north of Vire, infantry and a Cromwell tank moving through a taped gap in a minefield.

Corps, (9th and 10th SS Panzer Divisions), once again from east to west, from the Caen back to the Caumont sector. Using his considerable superiority and his control of the air, Montgomery was thus making Kluge dance entirely to his tune. It could not last long. The German front was near cracking. Individual German troops and units were fighting well, but the incessant air attacks and the freshness of their enemies combined to produce despair. Nevertheless the two newly-arrived SS Panzer divisions mounted some spirited attacks in the area of Vire and at Aunay-sur-Odon, forcing back 7th Armoured Division which had been deployed on the left of XXX Corps .

Meanwhile fresh British formations were brought up and a new phase of operations, a push on a broad front began. 3rd Division was deployed on the extreme right, east of Vire: and XII Corps came up of the left between XX Corps and Canadian First Army now responsible for the Caen sector. The Germans were still fighting for every yard on Second Army front which extended on a line from Caen to Vire. General Eberbach, commanding Panzer Group West, at this point told Kluge that the best step would be to withdraw to the Seine, to give up Normandy. No sensible German commander thought otherwise.

Montgomery now again advanced his left. On 8th August, II Canadian Corps, with 51st Division and 1st Polish Armoured Division, launched a major attack down the Caen-Falaise road, and during the following week 21 Army Group, from north and north-west, drove towards Falaise, which fell to the Canadians on 15th August.

By then the American Army was not far away to the south.

The very spot in the Allied front where Second Army was fighting against a desperate German defence had become a hinge. The American breakout south-west and east was under way. The American Third Army (General Patton) had burst from Avranches and driven on Mortain, south of Vire, where a hastily-assembled German counter-attack did little to impede them. Patton then drove east to Le Mans, south of Angers, and sent VIII (US) Corps westwards into Brittany. On 10th August American troops, driving east towards the Seine, swung north through Alencon towards Argentan, only 15 miles south of Falaise.

The German Seventh Army, which had been holding the central part of the front, together with Panzer Group West (renamed Fifth Panzer Army), now found themselves in a great salient. At the tip and on the north flank of that salient was 21 Army Group. As First Canadian and Second British Armies advanced, the salient became a pocket - the 'Falaise Gap'. To the south the German front was now ripped open. To avoid encirclement there could be no other course except flight to the east. Pounded from the air, suffering appalling casualties in men, horses and machines, with units and detachments surrounded and surrendering, cohesion gone, the great German retreat was under way. Kluge handed over command to Field Marshal Model. German losses in the Normandy fighting totalled more than 140,000 men.

The fighting in Normandy had been hard. Because of the nature of the terrain it had particularly demanded skilled infantry, and the Allied infantry , who bore the brunt of the casualties, were of uneven quality and inadequate in quantity. Of armour there was no shortage, but the terrain limited its

use, in the main, to short range tactical rather than ambitious operational movements. The superior effectiveness of German tanks and anti-tank gunnery was repeatedly demonstrated. The Allied massive superiority in artillery played a significant part in victory, as did the Allied logistic achievement in supplying an enormous force from a main base across the Channel, at first over beaches and by the use of the pre-constructed MULBERRY harbours. Above all, Allied command of the air governed the battlefield and produced a campaign in which only one side could move with impunity, and in which destruction on a terrible scale became the grim marker of every major battle.

The battle of Normandy may be regarded as over by 15th August, the fall of Falaise. Henceforth, for a while, the task was pursuit.

Overleaf Map
Battle of Normandy: The Breakout and Advance to the Seine, 1 - 20 August 1944.

Right
Infantry and carriers waiting to advance in a narrow lane south of Caumont.

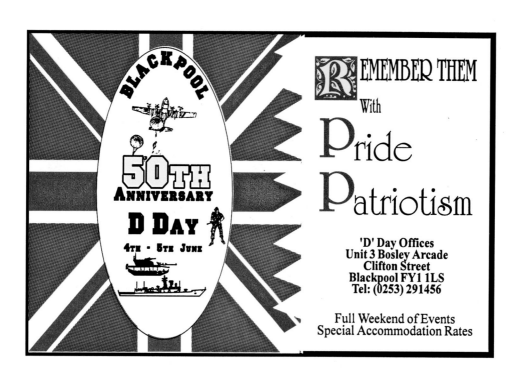

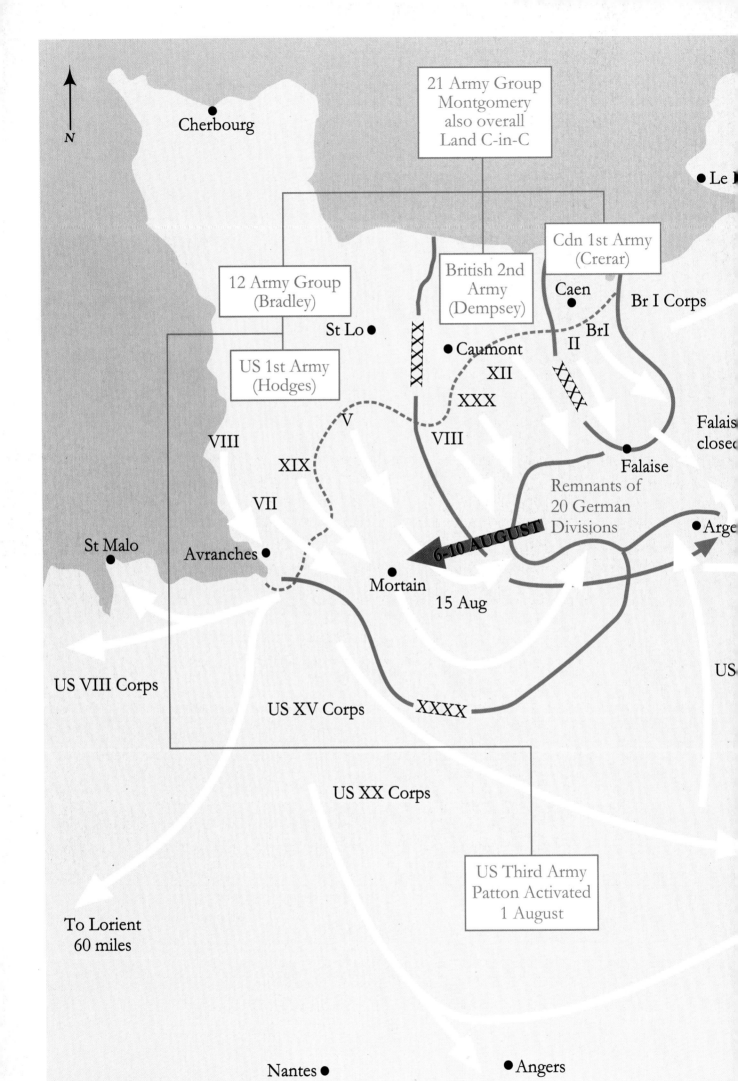

N

Cherbourg

21 Army Group
Montgomery
also overall
Land C-in-C

• Le

Cdn 1st Army
(Crerar)

British 2nd
Army
(Dempsey)

Caen

Br I Corps

12 Army Group
(Bradley)

St Lo •

• Caumont

BrI

II

XII

US 1st Army
(Hodges)

XXX

Falais
closed

V

VIII

VIII

XIX

Falaise

VII

Remnants of
20 German
Divisions

St Malo

Avranches •

• Arge

6-10 AUGUST

Mortain

15 Aug

US VIII Corps

US XV Corps

XXXX

US XX Corps

To Lorient
60 miles

US Third Army
Patton Activated
1 August

Nantes •

• Angers

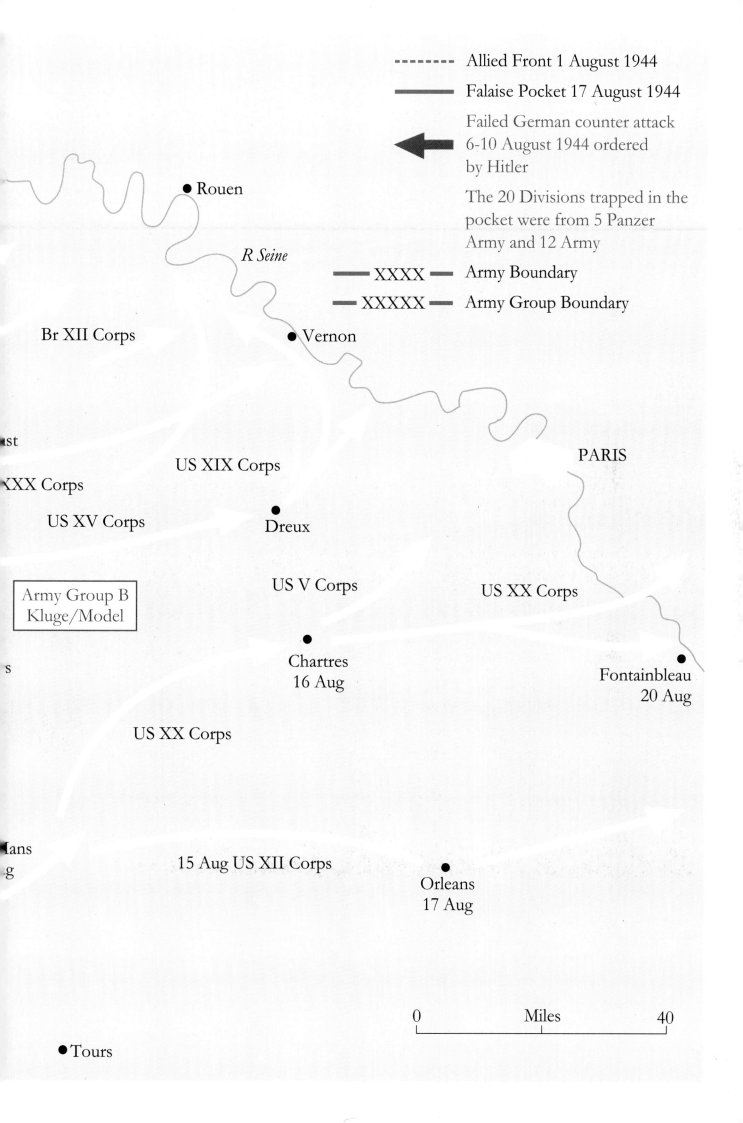

- - - - - - Allied Front 1 August 1944

———— Falaise Pocket 17 August 1944

Failed German counter attack
6-10 August 1944 ordered
by Hitler

The 20 Divisions trapped in the
pocket were from 5 Panzer
Army and 12 Army

—— XXXX —— Army Boundary

—— XXXXX —— Army Group Boundary

● Rouen

R Seine

Br XII Corps

● Vernon

PARIS

st

XXX Corps

US XIX Corps

US XV Corps

Dreux

US V Corps

US XX Corps

Army Group B
Kluge/Model

s

Chartres
16 Aug

Fontainbleau
20 Aug

US XX Corps

Ians

g

15 Aug US XII Corps

Orleans
17 Aug

0   Miles   40

● Tours

Give your business this extra competitive edge!

Are you first in your field? The Volunteer Reserve Forces could contribute to keeping you ahead. Reservists are trained to test their capabilities to the limit. They work for companies like yours, giving their spare time to help provide up to a quarter of the Nation's defence forces.

So what's that to you? Quite a lot if your competitors are employing them! The intensive training that men and women receive in the Reserve Forces has proved a valuable bonus to employers. Reservists are taught new technical and management skills; they develop initiative,

N E L C

THE VOLUNTEER RESERVE FORCES

self-reliance and leadership qualities and are fit and alert. All this at no cost to their companies!

That's why it pays to support Reservists on your staff. They become better employees and help give your business that extra competitive edge! For full information on how supporting the Volunteer Reserve Forces could help your company, contact:

The National Employers' Liaison Committee, Duke of York's HQ, Chelsea, London SW3 4SS. Tel: 071-218 4151.

ISSUED BY THE NATIONAL EMPLOYERS' LIAISON COMMITTEE
ON BEHALF OF THE TERRITORIAL ARMY AND THE VOLUNTEER RESERVES OF THE ROYAL NAVY, ROYAL MARINES AND THE ROYAL AIR FORCE

THEY ALSO SERVED

Throughout D-Day Salvation Army officers were on hand to minister to the physical and spiritual needs of His Majesty's Armed Forces – something they've been doing since 1895.

NORMANDY 1944

THE GULF 1991

From visiting the wounded and contacting relatives, to providing food and accommodation, or simply a cup of tea and a comforting word, The Salvation Army reaches out to those in need.

At home and abroad, during peacetime and in war, our officers offer help in the most practical and straightforward ways.

Such work is only possible thanks to those supporters of yesterday who remembered The Salvation Army in their wills. Legacies provide 40% of the income of The Salvation Army and make a vital contribution to our work with servicemen and women and their families. To find out how you can leave a legacy to The Salvation Army

PLEASE CALL

0800 108101

now and ask for our Legacy Promotions Officer, Mrs Lieut.-Colonel Doreen Caffull. Or write to her at: The Salvation Army, FREEPOST KE3466, 101 Queen Victoria Street, London EC4B 4SR.

Thank you and God bless you.

The Salvation Army 'A registered charity'.

BRITAIN'S ARMED FORCES TODAY

Fifty years have passed since British, US, Canadian and other Allied forces landed on the beaches of Normandy to initiate the liberation of Europe from Nazi domination.

In order to achieve this great feat Britain and America had to focus all their energies on maintaining immensely powerful armed forces and the civilian infrastructure to support them.

Clearly in 1994 we live in very different circumstances, particularly after the end of the Cold War. After the collapse of the Soviet Union and the removal of the massive military threat that Europe had faced for 40 years, it has been possible since 1990 to reduce military spending in the West and to make sensible cuts to the size of armed forces.

Taking 1985 as the baseline, and on the evidence of plans announced by December 1993, the changes should have the following effects by the middle of this decade:-

First, the United Kingdom will cut defence expenditure by somewhat under 22 per cent, compared with planned reductions in US defence expenditure of just over 20 per cent and in Germany of nearly 30 per cent.

Second, British defence expenditure should fall from 5.2 per cent of GDP in 1985 to 3 per cent in 1996, compared with a projected fall in United States military spending from 6.5 per cent to 3 per cent by 1998, in German from 3.2 per cent to 1.8 per cent (falling to 1.5 per cent by 1998), and in French from 4 per cent to 3 per cent.

Third, there should be similarly steep reductions in regular uniformed manpower. British military personnel will fall from 327,000 in 1985 to 246,000 by 1996 (a fall of 24 per cent), American from 3.1 million to 1.6 million (48 per cent), German 478,000 to about 390,000 (about 20 per cent), and French from 477,000 to about 390,000 (also about 20 per cent).

These statistics give only a partial picture of the radical force restructuring which has accompanied them. By about 1995 Britain will lose a fifth of its destroyers and frigates, all its diesel-powered submarines, more than a quarter of its infantry battalions, two-fifths of its armoured regiments and over a third of its military aircraft. The commitment to provide two well-equipped divisions, as well as the commander and a significant number of corps troops, for NATO's new Allied Command Europe Rapid Reaction Corps is a major challenge for an Army already stretched by the demands of restructuring and Northern Ireland.

Nevertheless, although Britain has undertaken a major force reduction exercise, it maintains the traditions of 1944 in all three armed services. Britain's Armed Forces today are highly professional, superbly equipped with the latest technology, and hardened by operational experience during the withdrawal from Empire in the 1945-75

period and more recently in the Falklands, in the Gulf and in Bosnia.

In the first two instances the Royal Navy, the Army and the Royal Air Force won great victories and in the third the Armed Forces are operating in the most difficult of circumstances with great determination. What is perhaps the most important characteristic of today's relatively-small armed forces is their flexibility. They must be capable of operating in an internal security role in Northern Ireland, a UN role in Bosnia, a conventional armoured role as the main contributors to the Allied Rapid Reaction Force, and in other theatres such as Norway, Belize, the Falklands and Hong Kong, as well as in the skies above and oceans surrounding these theatres. More than any other modern military organization, the British Armed Forces have shown a particular aptitude for such flexibility. Fifty years on Britain can be proud of its Armed Forces.

A soldier from 5 Airborne brigade silhouetted against a dawn sky as he advances over the Scottish hills. He is armed with an SA80 5.56mm assault rifle.

THE ROLE OF THE TORNADO GR1

General George S Patton's aphorism, *"The only sure defence is offence"* is as pertinent today as it was when he coined it 50 years ago. Indeed, offensive action is particularly relevant to air operations since it exploits one of the most potent characteristics of air power - the ability to strike targets deep in enemy territory. For over 10 years the mainstay of the RAF's offensive power has been the versatile and extremely capable Tornado GR1.

The Tornado is a two-seat, variable-geometry, fly-by-wire aircraft optimised for low-level operations in the central region in all weathers by day or night.

Its versatility is general purpose bombs, cluster munitions, laser guided bombs (LGBs) and , uniquely, the JP233 runway cratering and airfield denial weapon. The aircraft can also deliver the Air-Launched Anti Radiation Missile (ALARM) for suppression of enemy air defences (SEAD).

The Tornado air defence variant is responsible for security of United Kingdom airspace. Recently it has also been deployed in Italy to help police the United Nations imposed no-fly zone over Bosnia.

The Tornado is adaptable enough to be used for any of the offensive roles of airpower - including close air support should the operational situation so demand. However, the aircraft is particularly well suited to the offensive

counter-air and air interdiction roles since these best exploit the Tornado's excellent range and weapon carriage capability.

History has shown that control of the air is of crucial importance not only to air operations but also to virtually all types of surface and sub-surface operations as well. The more formidable the opposing air power, the more important achieving control of the air becomes.

Thus, the counter-air campaign will always take priority over other air campaigns. It follows therefore that, at least at the outset of hostilities, the most likely use for the Tornado would be in support of the counter-air campaign. In tasking terms, this would translate into employing Tornado for attack of airfields - primarily with JP233 - and for SEAD missions using ALARM.

Once the required degree of control of the air had been achieved, missions in excess of those needed to maintain it could then be diverted to tasks in support of other strategic, operational or tactical objectives as required.

The RAF currently has four Tornado GR1 squadrons with a primary role of overland strike-attack. Two further squadrons are presently in the process of converting to the maritime attack role using the Sea Eagle anti-ship missile. In

addition, the RAF also operates two specialist reconnaissance squadrons which are equipped with the Tornado GR1A. Both the maritime and recce squadrons have a secondary role of ground attack.

When the aircraft was conceived in the late1960s, the precedents for the aircraft did not augur well. The previous 10 years had seen the demise of many national aircraft projects, culminating in the cancellation of the TSR-2 because of growing budgetary pressures. The proposed purchase of the American F-111 as a cheaper, off-the-shelf replacement was to share the same fate. Yet it was increasingly obvious that no European nation could hope to develop and fund a major military aircraft on its own. It was against this backdrop that the imperatives for the UK to develop a multi-role aircraft in collaboration with European partners emerged and which eventually led to the requirement for the Tornado.

Nevertheless, persistent pressures on the Defence Budget ensured that the project was subjected to severe scrutiny well into the '70s.

Indeed, that the Tornado survived in the face of continuing budgetary difficulties was probably only because the implications of cancelling an international venture of such magnitude were politically unacceptable.

Tornado GR1 aircraft re-fuel from a VC-10 tanker during the Gulf War. RAF Tornado's performed the crucial and unique role of low level attack against Iraqi airforce bases using the JP233 runway cratering and airfield denial weapon.

Despite these early problems, and a steady trickle of critics who continued to snipe at the aircraft throughout it's 14 years of development, the first two Tornados were delivered to the Tri-National Tornado Training Establishment at RAF Cottesmore in June 1979. In 1982, the aircraft began to enter front line service in earnest.

The Tornado force rapidly built up as nine GR1 squadrons were equipped, manned and , after an appropriate work-up period, declared as operational to NATO at a rate of one every three months.

This would represent an ambitious programme for any modern aircraft but, given the complexity of the Tornado, it was quite startling. Success in international competitions and exercises swiftly followed and proved that the weapon-aiming and delivery system was capable of achieving previously unheard-of levels of accuracy.

By August of 1990 when the Gulf crisis erupted, the nine Tornado GR1 had gained almost five years experience of being at the forefront of NATO's strike-attack capability. Only the two GR1A squadrons, dealing with teething problems with their brand new equipment, remained to be declared in their primary role of recce.

As the UN deadline of 15th January approached, it became increasingly plain that the Tornado force was about to get its operational debut, not in the skies over Europe for which it had been designed and trained, but in the Gulf - a very different theatre indeed. By the start of the war, the RAF had deployed a force of over 40 Tornado GR1s to the Gulf in three squadron-sized detachments.

General Buster Glosson, Director of Operations at HQ Central Air Force in Riyadh, was responsible to General Chuck Horner for developing the air campaign and General Glosson made it quite clear that he wanted to pit Coalition strengths against Iraqi weaknesses.

For him this meant fighting the war at night, at least at the outset. In terms of numbers, the Iraqis possessed a formidable air force and this had to be countered. The Coalition was short of effective airfield denial weapons and so it fell naturally to the Tornados armed with JP233 to take on the task of attacking Iraqi airfields at night.

Iraqi airfields were simply too numerous and the main operating bases (MOBs) physically too big for the available force to have a realistic expectation of closing all of the potential targets. Instead, General Glosson settled for the lesser aim of disrupting air operations at selected MOBs rather than preventing them altogether. In the event, the Coalition counter air campaign was more effective than could have been hoped and after four nights the air opposition had been effectively neutralised. Tornados had made a significant contribution by closing eight Iraqi airfields and damaging several more.

But with air superiority firmly established, it made no sense for the bombers to remain at low level where Iraqi anti-aircraft fire posed the sole remaining major threat to their survival. Therefore, on 21st January the GR1s shifted emphasis to meduim-level operations. The original concept, once JP233 operations were complete, had been for the Tornados to deliver LGBs with American aircraft providing the laser designation.

In the event however all suitable American assets were engaged in 'SCUD hunting'. Hence, for the next 10 days the Tornados attacked area targets such as oil refineries with unguided 1000-lb bombs. The aircraft was not designed for medium-level operations of this type and, not surprisingly, results were mixed.

However, on 28th January the first six Buccaneers of a force that was eventually to total 12 aircraft arrived in theatre to provide a laser-designation capability for the Tornados. Medium level bombing results were soon transformed. By 2nd February, the mixed force was ready for operations and on that date two Buccaneers and four Tornados successfully attacked a road bridge over the Euphrates with LGBs. From that point, the emphasis shifted from the area to pinpoint targets and over the next three weeks the Tornados supported by Buccaneers attacked many of the bridges over the Euphrates and Tigris.

As the success of the Coalition interdiction effort grew, and consequently the number of bridges left undamaged decreased, the focus began to move back again onto enemy air assets.

From 12th February onwards, the Tornados and Buccaneers were tasked increasingly against enemy hardened aircraft shelters (HAS) and other airbase infrastructure.

On its own, the available Buccaneer force had the capacity to laser-designate for about 60 per cent of the Tornados. The remainder had to continue to operate against area targets with unguided bombs. However, on 6th February, the Tornado acquired its own laser designation capability when two prototype thermal imaging and laser designation pods (TIALD) arrived in theatre. TIALD offered many advantages over the older Pavespike system used by the Buccaneer, including a night capability. On 10th February, after a brief work-up based upon the Buccaneer experience, TIALD was used operationally for the first time. Within a week, the whole Tornado force was using LGBs and unguided bombing ceased.

Contrary to the impression created by the media, less than 20 per cent of the total bomb tonnage dropped in the Gulf by Coalition forces involved precision-guided munitions (PGMs) such as LGBs. Yet those that were delivered accounted for about 80 per cent of the critical damage inflicted. That figure would have been even more impressive had not more than a quarter of all PGM missions been aborted due to poor weather. The conclusion for future weapons procurement is self-evident.

As the date designated for the start of the ground war approached, senior Coalition commanders were determined to ensure that the Iraqi air Force would be in no position to make a last ditch attempt to support its army. Consequently, in one final change of emphasis, the Tornado force was used from 18th February onwards to close all of the airbases near to the battlefield. Thus, the Tornado GR1 finished the war as it had started, attacking runways in support of the offensive counter-air campaign, albeit employing very different tactics and weapons.

The war saw many 'firsts' for the Tornado. Of particular note was the part played by the GR1A recce variant. Following a hectic week of final modifications to the recce equipment, six GR1As were rushed to the Gulf on 14th January and they flew their first war mission four nights later.

The aircraft provided the Coalition with an important low-level night capability and it made a contribution out of all proportion to the size of the detachment - particularly when bad weather interfered with many other systems.

General Glosson acknowledged that at such times the GR1As were his only source of tactical battle damage assessment. Another 'first' was the use of ALARM. The missile was accelerated into RAF service just before the war began and the 100-plus rounds fired during hostilities achieved a creditable 75 per cent success rate.

In all, the Tornado GR1s flew over 1,500 sorties at a cost of five aircraft lost in action, four during the low-level phase. The low-level attrition rate of about 1 per cent was an order of magnitude higher than that suffered by the rest of the coalition forces and there can be little doubt that the low-level environment is inherently dangerous - especially for aircraft that must overfly the target in order to deliver their weapons.

However, low-level operations were largely independent of the weather, an important consideration in many other theatres. Furthermore, some low-level bombing missions did achieve surprise and many more could have done so had not the support package at medium level stimulated the defences into action long before the Tornado force had been detected.

It is worth noting that, in contrast to the GR1's experience, the recce detachment flew unsupported, at low level, throughout the entire war - a total of about 140 sorties - without loss.

General McPeak, the Chief of Staff of the USAF, put into context the significance of the Gulf War to military doctrine when he said shortly after the conflict was over, *"This is the first time in history that a field army has been defeated by air power."* Few would argue that, given the unique nature of the Gulf War, we would be wise to exercise caution when we apply its lessons. Nevertheless, the conflict remains the strongest validation yet of the doctrine of offensive action. It highlighted the decisive importance of using air power primarily as an offensive rather than defensive weapon under all but the most unfavourable operational conditions. But, although having the correct strategy is vital, it will count for little without effective weapon systems, people and training, at all levels, to translate theory into action. The Tornado force confirmed under combat conditions that it possesses a potent offensive capability. A stand-off weapon and all-weather PGM would enhance that capability immeasurably. The qualitative edge provided by the right equipment in the hands of the right people with the right training contributed to the swift and decisive victory in the Gulf.

It is an edge that must be maintained as we look to the 21st Century.

138

MONTY ?

Monty or Clifton James ? Vodka or Wyborowa ?

It's easy to make the mistake. Many people were fooled during World War 2 by Clifton James who doubled for Monty.

After tasting Wyborowa you will not be fooled by other vodkas.

Wyborowa pure grain vodka and the Wyborowa family of flavoured vodkas.

Wyborowa and friends - Remember the name. Don't forget the taste.

WÓDKA WYBOROWA

Wiśniówka
CHERRY VODKA

COMMAND, CONTROL AND COMMUNICATIONS

'Few operations and campaigns can ever be expected to proceed as planned. Success depends, therefore, on effective command and control being exercised at every stage. Effective command and control depends on centralized command and exercising it from the highest practicable level and decentralized execution'.[1]

It has long been recognised that effective command, control and communications (C3) are essential to the successful prosecution of war and, historically, their critical importance was certainly highlighted during the run up to D-Day. But, despite the great strikes that had been achieved throughout the Second World War, C3 during that conflict still relied very much on 'line of sight'.

Over the ensuing years great progress has been made; that said, the need for high-level unitary command of air forces - while adopting a closely integrated system for their employment and targeting - is still as valid in the age of satellite communications and stealth technology as it was when the Allies landed on the beaches of Normandy in 1944.

Air power assets have the ability to be concentrated rapidly so as to provide mass to overwhelm an enemy whether as part of a joint campaign or independently. In this, air power's attributes of quick response and flexibility mean that

1 AP3000, 2nd edition, Air Power Doctrine Manual

140

The joint surveillance target and attack radar system (JSTARS) in flight. This system was used to great effect against Iraqi ground targets during the Gulf War. It enabled allied forces to control the battlefield to an unprecedented degree.

it must be coordinated if it is to achieve maximum effectiveness. The necessary planning and coordination of an air campaign certainly requires a comprehensive and flexible C3 system but, while the individual elements are vital in themselves, it is the way in which they are brought together into the one integrated whole that contributes so much to success. The most recent example of this is the Gulf War.

It was the Allies C3 system (together with the intelligence support) that allowed them to take the initiative in the Gulf. The system had to be built up as Allied Forces deployed and eventually it had to cope with over 800,000 personnel from 36 nations with dozens of different weapons systems and unprecedented levels of demand.[2]

COMMAND AND CONTROL

Command and control hinged around unity of command; to provide unity in such difficult circumstances with so many nations involved a Coalition Coordination Communications and Integration Centre (CCCIC) was formed. General Norman Schwarzkopf had command of all US forces in theatre and had operational control of forces from the UK, France, Italy and Canada; while Prince Khalid , Sultan of Saudi Arabia,had command of Saudi forces and operational control of the forces from Afghanistan, Bahrain, Bangladesh, Egypt, Kuwait, Morocco, Niger, Oman, Pakistan, Qatar, Senegal, Syria and the UAE. (Operational control means that a higher formation has control over a unit's activities but no responsibility for administration and logistics support.)

Decentralized execution was vital and depended on secure communications with redundancy. Control was conducted through the use of a daily Air Tasking Order (ATO) which detailed the task and broad mission plans. Details of in-flight refuelling towlines, call signs, radio frequencies, times, locations, altitudes, targets and munitions were provided for over 1000 sorties per day. While the ATO had its drawbacks - principally because it lacked flexibility - it was the only realistic method of coordinating the enormous air effort provided by so many different forces.

As the size of the UK's forces has reduced and we are no longer able to deploy regional commanders-in-chief our national military doctrine argues that the essential analysis and planning should be conducted at an appropriate four-star headquarters; the sheer size of the Command and Control requirements during the Gulf War meant that Strike Command's Headquarters was the only one that could meet the planning and support requirements for our joint forces deployed. Within the joint HQ, day-to-day monitoring of the conflict was undertaken by a battle management group which was run by a two-star Director of Operations. This concept freed the in-theatre commander to concentrate on operational detail.

Exercising overall command and control in such circumstances provided complex challenges for a multi-cultural, multi-national force where there was no existing C2 organization, no agreed common practices, and where there were different requirements and perceptions of Rules of Engagement. While this was achieved with conspicuous success, it is noteworthy that this was the first time that such a problem had needed to be addressed since the Second World War. As in previous conflicts, the difficulties could only be overcome if effective communications were possible.

COMMUNICATIONS

All forms were vital to success and, in particular, space-based communications were crucial. Military satellites provided strategic and tactical communications facilities for ground and air forces and at the height of the conflict 86 per cent of all communications was via military satellite.[3] The satellites operate in the UHF, SHF and EHF frequency ranges and so provide a wide bandwidth and high capacity. Early communications satellites operated in a low orbit and so were only in view of ground stations for a relatively short period; this led to poor performance. Current military communications satellites are placed in a geostationary orbit to provide worldwide coverage with three satellites and reduce the need for ground station tracking. There is now a move towards the use of onboard processing to permit satellite-to-satellite transmission so reducing the ground processing requirement yet further and also reducing the overall number of ground stations required.

At the time of the Iraqi invasion of Kuwait, Britain had only three Defence Communications Satellites available. They proved inadequate for the task and sufficient communications capability was available only when these were supplemented by US systems. The problem centred around having to service six different locations in the Gulf and provide multiple cross-links. Additionally, C2 elements which were spread out in Riyadh needed to be linked and the fact that the port of Al Jubail formed the logistic centre with army elements being located up to 600 kilometres away compounded the problem. Moreover, the British Army's 'PTARMIGAN' tactical communications system had to be integrated into the SATCOM network.

In the air, there was a need for non-jammable, air-to-air communications and 'Have Quick' frequency-agile, secure radios were installed in all aircraft. Air-to-air engagements were controlled wherever possible by Boeing E-3A AWACS aircraft although, at times, the volume of traffic made it impossible to offer a service to every potential user. These all placed additional demands on the network.

One of the newer systems to make its debut during the Gulf Conflict was the Boeing E-8 Joint STARS (Surveillance Target Attack Radar System). JSTARS is designed to detect, classify and track moving or stationary vehicles over the battlefield and to transmit that information in real time to the operational army and air force commands. The system worked remarkably well. For example, on 22nd January 1991 JSTARS located a division assembly area and a 60-vehicle armoured convoy moving towards Kuwait; and an air strike was ordered which resulted in the destruction of 59 of the tanks. JSTARS proved to be a most effective asset and complemented the AWACS to the extent that every moving target on or over the battlefield could be monitored continuously by coalition forces.

2 "Conduct of the Persian Gulf Conflict: An Interim Report to Congress" Congressional Research Service, Washington, 1991, page 15-1.

3 US Secretary of the Air Force Donald B Rice, 7 th may 1991 in speech to the Washington Strategy Seminar.

Of course, the US, too, needed considerably more capacity than was routinely available. The major US communications network is the Defence Satellite Communications System (DSCS) which provided global wide-band communications for the US Department of Defence and other government agencies. Currently, the system utilises two types of satellite. For the future, however, the US is developing the Military Strategic Tactical and Relay (MILSTAR) programme with the aim of providing a worldwide, highly jam-resistant, survivable and enduring satellite communications capability. These satellites will operate in the EHF frequency range and use increased on-board processing, nuclear-hardened electronic components and techniques designed to reduce vulnerability to laser weapons. As a result, the system will provide considerable protection against both Electronic Counter Measures (ECM) and physical attack. Each satellite will also have direct cross-links to other satellites in the constellation which will reduce dependence on ground stations.

In addition to the US and UK systems, two satellites launched in 1970 and 1971 form a NATO communications system. These were replaced by three satellites between 1976 and 1978 with a fourth being launched in 1984. The system is funded by NATO and is fully compatible with the US DSCS. It represents the world's second largest military communications satellite system with a ground segment comprising one mobile and 22 static terminals. Elements of this system, too, were pressed into service during the Gulf Conflict.

The other major West European military satellite communications systems is the French SYRACUSE network. This differs from the previous systems as it is not based on independent, single mission satellites but, instead, incorporates the military requirement within commercial satellites.

UTILIZATION OF SATELLITE INFORMATION

In addition to communications, the main roles performed by military satellites are: to provide accurate navigation information to ground units; to supply surveillance of an enemy using photographic, radar, infra-red and electronic sensors; and to provide meteorological data for use by weather forecasters.

Throughout the Gulf War extensive use was made of surveillance satellites. In the early days they revealed the essentially-defensive posture of the Iraqi forces thus allaying the initial fear of an attack against Saudi Arabia. Moreover, they provided highly-accurate targeting information which was used to plan air and ground attacks and to programme Tomahawk cruise missiles. This enabled attacking forces to plan accurately and complete attacks whilst limiting collateral damage. The presence of television news teams and other civilians within the combat zone made the limitation of civilian casualties a high priority if domestic support for the war within Coalition nations was to be maintained.

Surveillance satellites also provided post-raid battle damage assessment so reducing the requirement for reconnaissance aircraft overflights. Additionally, satellite date was used to produce up-to-date maps of Kuwait and Saudi Arabia, an urgent requirement because of the inadequacy of the maps available at the time of initial deployment.

Early warning surveillance satellites and meteorological satellites were also used extensively. The former gave vital warning of SCUD missile launches, so alerting the PATRIOT batteries and enabling timely interception. Satellite meteorological data was used to generate accurate weather forecasts for use by Alliance commanders. This information was par-

ticularly important when precision-guided weapons were to be used as, in that case, target visibility was essential if laser designation was to be successful. Satellite meteorological imagery was also used to determine the moisture content of the soil and thus identify the routes that would support the weight of the armoured forces for the attack on Iraq. And, finally, had Iraq resorted to the use of chemical weapons, weather information would have been vital for tracking chemicals and forecasting when the they would dissipate.

Accurate navigation in desert regions in particular has always presented a problem. Fortunately, over recent years satellites have been deployed which can greatly assist the traveller. The NAVSTAR Global Positioning Systems (GPS) allows users on land, sea or in the air to determine their position anywhere on the Earth's surface with an accuracy of 16 metres in three dimensions. Relative GPS was thus very useful in that it allowed users to converge at a given point by following their own lightweight and inexpensive, hand-held receiver systems. Very few were available at the outset but, by the end of the Gulf Conflict, more than 4,000 were in use (including 2,700 hand-held units). Their expensive use again highlighted the need for up-to-date maps and charts; many of the Gulf Region were far too inaccurate to be of use when such levels of accuracy are demanded.The Gulf Conflict confirmed that in modern warfare any mobile force deployed away from base facilities must have access to a satellite com-

munications systems that can be rapidly re-orientated and enhanced to cover a particular area of interest if effective C3 is to be possible.

In addition, those forces must be capable of using commercial satellite communications systems to overcome any deficiencies in the military capability, and they must be equipped with an adequate number of lightweight, mobile communication and meteorological ground stations.

Finally, GPS receivers must be available for all aircraft and vehicles and lightweight, hand-held receivers are essential pieces of equipment for ground troops.

'High technology' has always given a qualitative edge and it remains vitally important in modern warfare. The Gulf Conflict, in particular, gave a special insight into importance of high-technology C3 and intelligence systems.

Coalition forces used their state-of-the-art equipment with devastating effect; by way of contrast, the Iraqi C3 network - their eyes, ears and voice - was destroyed within the first 24 hours of the conflict. Thereafter, the outcome was inevitable.

That lesson should not go unheeded.

BBC

"...this record of dispatches broadcast by the BBC's War Correspondents...give[s] an interesting and vivid account of the progress of the campaign in North-western Europe from the beaches of Normandy to the Shores of the Baltic; and, when the history of the times comes to be written, they will prove of great value and importance."

Reproduced by kind permission of A. P. Watt Ltd.

B. L. Montgomery
Field-Marshal, Commander-in-Chief
British Army of the Rhine.

These words were written by Field Marshal Montgomery in November 1945 in his forward to *War Report*, a unique record of dispatches broadcast by the BBC's War Correspondents with the Allied Expeditionary Force from 6 June 1944-5 May 1945.

The BBC played a vital part in bringing up-to-the-minute, graphic accounts of events to the listening public during the war years, as it still does today.

To commemorate the 50th Anniversary of the D-Day Landings, the BBC is reproducing *War Report,* an historic record of BBC correspondent's war dispatches. Also available from UK stockists are *The D-Day Landings, Victory in Europe* and *The Second World War* in a complete collection of audio and video cassettes. The book and recordings are a testament to the BBC War Correspondents and a rare document of history.

BBC
ENTERPRISES

CLOSE AIR AND NAVAL GUNFIRE SUPPORT

Close air support has come a long way since 1944. Although the size of the force available today for this role is far smaller than it was 50 years ago, the aircraft are far more capable. They carry more effective weapons, they deliver them with greater precision and they can do so in marginal weather conditions. There are currently two aircraft types of ground attack aircraft in the inventory of the RAF, the Anglo-French Jaguar and the BAe Harrier.

The British Aerospace Harrier Mark 2 GR7 night attack variant made its maiden flight in November 1989 and entered service with the Royal Airforce in the early 1990's. It is equipped with a forward looking infra red sensor, digitial electronic map display and the pilot is equipped with night vision goggles. Together these systems allow high speed, low level attacks on heavily defended targets at night.

The Jaguar began to arrive in the front line during 1974, and the last of the 200 machines produced for the Royal Air Force was delivered three years later. Interestingly, the Jaguar was first conceived as an advanced trainer, but during development it was realised that an attack capability would also be valuable, and eventually this operational role became the more important. With uprated twin engines, this version became the standard Jaguar GR1A for the direct tactical support of ground forces.

Two 30mm Aden cannons are carried internally beneath the nose of the aircraft, and there are five hard-points for stores, one on the centre-line and two under each wing. They can be used to carry free-fall or retarded bombs, cluster bombs, rockets, or auxiliary fuel tanks.

Alternatively, the centre-line point can accommodate a reconnaissance pod, and in addition the Jaguar can take a Sidewinder air-to-air missile on each wing-tip for self-protection. During the Gulf war in 1991, some Jaguars were also fitted with Electronic Counter Measures (ECM) pods and with Phimat chaff dispensers.

Three years before the Jaguar entered service, the first Harriers had arrived in the front line. Since then, the type has been so much improved that the present variant, the GR7, is not merely another mark of Harrier, but a totally new aircraft. The cockpit of the Harrier is one of the most advanced in the world today. There is a very wide-angle head-up display for the pilot, together with a Forward-Looking Infra-Red sensor, a moving map display, a suite of Electronic Warfare equipment and,

A Jaguar GR Mark 1 from number 6 Squadron Royal airforce armed with two Sidewinder AIM9L Air to Air missiles. This aircraft was deployed by the Royal Air Force is Bosnia in support of United Nations.

shortly to be added to the whole fleet, a Global Positioning-Inertial Navigation fit. Together, these systems offer an unrivalled ability to find and to strike targets in poor weather and even by night, this last being a remarkable step forward for the close air support mission.

But most impressive of all is the punch that the GR7 can deliver. There are two under-fuselage packs, each mounting a 30mm cannon, and between them is a hard-point designed to accept 1000lb of stores. There is also a total of eight under-wing hard-points for auxiliary fuel, for ECM chaff or flare pods, or for weapons. The latter can include for example Sidewinder, Magic or Maverick missiles, up to 16 540lb free-fall or retarded bombs, twelve BL755 or similar cluster bombs, ten Paveway laser-guided bombs, ten SNEB rocket pods or gun pods.

Because it can take off in only a few yards and land vertically, the Harrier GR7 can be based close to the scene of operations, thus offering a very fast response to tasking by ground forces. It can even operate from ships. Together with its all-round performance and its ability to strike hard and with great precision, the Harrier GR7 is at the forefront of today's ground attack aircraft

NAVAL GUNFIRE SUPPORT IN THE FALKLANDS AND GULF WARS

Naval bombardment of Argentinian shore positions was a key part of the Royal Navy's operations in the war to recapture the Falkland Islands in 1982.

In all, over 8,000 rounds, (well over 220 tons of ordance), were fired by the Task Force in shore bombardment operations, over 1000 of them by HMS Avenger and more than 900 by HMS Arrow. From as early as 1st May, well before the start of the landings of the main British forces in San Carlos water on 21stMay, destroyers and frigates regularly shelled enemy positions, mostly during the hours of darkness. Besides the considerable material damage and casualties inflicted, the bombardments had a serious effect on Argentinian morale: most of their key positions on the islands were well within the range of the British 4.5 inch guns, and they were subjected to up to 300 rounds each weighing 55 pounds, during each ship's spell on the "gun line".

During the night immediately preceding the amphibious assault, a demonstration was mounted by HMS Glamorgan with starshell and high explosive, to confuse and divert the enemy attention from the landings.

Until sufficient guns had been landed for the attacking force, their only heavy weapons were the bombs of the Sea Harriers and the shells fired by the naval escorts.

In the land campaign, every major assault by British ground troops was supported by naval gunfire. During the advance to Goose Green by 2 Para, for example, the effect of over 150 shells from HMS Arrow had a devastating effect on the defenders, and played a key part in the planning for the major set-piece battles which finally ejected the Argentinians from their strong positions in the heights around Port Stanley. For the attacks on Mount Harriet, Two Sisters, Wireless Ridge and Mount Longdon, each objective was allocated a destroyer or frigate in addition a six-gun RA battery of 105mm pieces.

The value of naval gunfire in support of land forces had been so convincingly demonstrated that the last batch Type 22 frigates had the tried and effective Mark 8 gun incorporated into their design, and since then it has been the Ministry of Defence policy to include guns for shore bombardment in all future designs of frigates and destroyers.

In the Gulf War, the geography and enemy dispositions did not lend themselves to the employment of naval gunfire support so readily as in the Falklands. Initially, the 16-inch guns of the US battleships Missouri and Wisconsin had the ability to stand off and deliver shells at over 20 miles range, usually

spotted by an unmanned aircraft. However, the speed of the Iraqi surrender in Kuwait precluded the planned naval gunfire support from Royal Navy destroyers. In the Gulf, shore bombardment using precision-guided cruise missiles provided the ability to strike land targets accurately from the sea at ranges of hundreds of miles.

In the uncertain world of the future, where power projection from the sea is likely to become more, rather than less, important, the provision of naval gunfire support will continue to be a key role for maritime forces.

Naval gunfire support was extensively used by the Royal Navy during the Falklands campaign to shell Argentinian positions. Both US and Royal Navy ships also obombarded Iraqi shore positions during the Gulf War. Here a Royal Navy ship bombards a distant target.

SUBMARINES IN THE ROYAL NAVY TODAY

The Royal Navy's submarine arm today consists of two nuclear-powered seagoing components: the strategic deterrent submarines of the VANGUARD and RESOLUTION Classes, and the 13 hunter-killer boats, SSNs. HMS Vanguard, the first of the Trident boats, is on schedule for operational deployment around the turn of this year.

The fourth boat has been ordered and the second and third, HMS Victorious and Vigilant, are progressing well. The Secretary of State of Defence recently announced that, on the basis of our current minimum defence needs, each submarine will deploy with no more than 96 warheads, and may carry significantly fewer. Four boats will guarantee that one is always at sea.

The recent dramatic changes in the international security situation, including the rapid decline in size and operating activity of the former Soviet Fleet has reduced the likely scale of our ASW operations in the North Atlantic. As a result, it has been decided to withdraw the UPHOLDER Class of conventional submarines from service by 1995, and concentrate on the proven capabilities of an all nuclear-powered force.

The modern nuclear submarine is not only an ideal platform from which to conduct warfare against opposing submarine and surface forces: with its particular qualities such as stealth, endurance (up to three months unsupported), survivability, ability to sustain high speed, and range of political, strategic or operational roles not provided by other platforms.

A Vanguard class SSBN on the surface. This boat has carried Britain's Polaris Ballistic missile system for many years.

For example, the despatch of an SSN in advance of a task group to an area of instability or potential conflict enables early insertion of special forces, and/or intelligence gathering. Once those activities which require the submarine to be covert are complete, it can be deployed in the traditional roles of sea denial and control. The Falklands campaign provided a graphic example of the ability of nuclear submarines to render virtually impotent a potentially dangerous naval opponent.

In the operations which seem to be most likely in the future, the SSN will be able to provide our government with a powerful instrument of political persuasion in areas of potential or actual conflict. The capacity of the submarine to undertake all these non anti-submarine warfare tasks does not detract from its abilities in the open oceans to shadow, and if necessary, sink anything on or below the surface of the sea, and to provide protection for the Trident force or other deployed groups.

Submarines are one of the three major components which enable the Royal Navy to meet its obligations to discharge the Defence Roles set out in the government White Paper, "Defending Our Future". Together with aircraft carriers and amphibious forces they are the principal components of maritime power.

MINE COUNTERMEASURES OPERATIONS BY THE ROYAL NAVY DURING THE GULF WAR

A crucial part of the Royal Navy's contribution to the success of Coalition naval operations in the Gulf War was that of mine countermeasures (MCM). The Iraqis were able to deploy not only relatively unsophisticated contact mines, but also modern influence mines. Many hundreds of such mines were laid using surface and air platforms, with the aim of disrupting the Coalition' sea lines of communication and of protecting their seaward flank from amphibious assault. Some contact mines also drifted, floating down the Gulf to provide

an additional hazard.

After an extensive work-up period covering all aspects of possible threats, such as NBCD (Nuclear, Biological, Chemical and Damage Control), and air and missile attacks, the RN mine countermeasures force moved into the waters of the Northern Persian Gulf in December 1991. The RN initially deployed HM Ships *Hurworth, Cattistock, Ledbury, Atherstone,* and *Dulverton* supported by the survey vessel HMS Herald and later by HMS Hecla.

They worked closely with the US Navy in the Northern Gulf and proved themselves extremely capable and reliable; in particular, the ability of the HUNT Class vessels to employ different mine countermeasures techniques, minesweeping, mine hunting, and the use of divers, was most valuable. The force was backed up by elements of the Fleet Diving Units based in the Landing Ship, Sir Galahad.

An important secondary task for the RN MCM force was to conduct hydrographic surveys of key sea areas, particularly approaches to ports, and of potential amphibious landing locations. Throughout the war, the RN MCM contingent operated in areas of extreme danger and provided a vital service in protecting Coalition shipping.

Many mines were destroyed, and hundreds of mine-like objects such as oil drums had to be checked. The success of the mine countermeasures operations was vital to the Coalition strategy, as they facilitated the naval gunfire support by the American battleships, and persuaded the enemy that the Allies intended to use the safe approaches for their amphibious assault force; while sustaining the seaward threat on the Iraqi ground forces left flank, two USN ships were damaged by mines.

No less vital has been the work since the war to clear the remaining ordnance. Following the end of the land battle, three more HUNT class minesweepers, *Brocklesby, Brecon* and *Bicester,* carried on the mine clearance effort. Conditions were far from ideal: the retreating Iraqi soldiers had ignited over 500 oil wells, and had damaged marine oil terminals, with resultant pollution in the form of thick oil slicks stretching many miles along the coast line.

The sky was black with oily smoke from the fires. This produced such poor water clarity that the RCMDS, the remote controlled mine disposal system, was unable to operate and clearance had to be carried out by divers.

The first task was to clear the unswept channels, approaches, and the coastal waters leading to Shuwaikh, Kuwait's main harbour, to allow supplies to enter the country. In the four-month period after hostilities *Brocklesby* alone cleared more than 50 mines.

Royal Navy divers also worked ashore to assist with mines that had come adrift from their moorings and had drifted on to the beaches. Working alongside the USN and Royal Australian Navy, the teams discovered more than 30 contact mines and many tonnes of other exploded ordance.

Mine counter measures throughout OPERATION GRANBY showed that the tactical procedures devised by the Royal Navy in peacetime, together with wide operational experience, - including the Suez Canal, and previous Persian Gulf operations, - and backed by demanding and realistic training, have provided the Royal Navy with a most effective and vital capability. The ability to provide safe passage for friendly forces in the face of a mine threat is one which a maritime nation, such as the United Kingdom, ignores at its peril.

LYNX OPERATIONS DURING THE GULF WAR

The sea Skua missile, fired from Royal Navy shipborne helicopters, was first used in action during the Falklands Campaign of 1982, when three targets, Alferez, Soberal, Rio Carcarana and Rio Iguazu, were engaged and put out of action. A total of eight Sea Skua missiles were fired and all were assessed to have hit their targets.

In the Gulf War, RN Lynx Mk 3s, deployed by all RN frigates and destroyers, demonstrated their multi-role capability and effectiveness, being described by one sea area commander as "surgical scalpels in amongst a good deal of raw firepower".

The aircraft were modified to improve their performance in the Gulf environment; cooling packages for gearboxes allowed the aircraft to operate in very hot ambient conditions while still retaining single-engine performance to hover and land. Extra equipment carried included a precision navigation system, a heavy machine gun, and state-of-the-art sensors.

Before hostilities commenced, RN Lynx helicopters operated in support of the embargo, the terms of the UN Resolutions 661 and 665, by identifying and interrogating merchant shipping over civilian radio bands. Suspect vessels were boarded from the helicopter, using rapid roping techniques perfected by the Royal Marines. Operations in these areas allowed the aircrew to become familiar with the geography and terrain of the southern to mid-Gulf territory.

Along with embargo patrols, preparations for a looming war continued. It was planned that the Lynx would operate alongside USN SH-60 helicopters, and cooperative tactics were devised and practised.

After the start of hostilities, the speed of reaction of the Lynx aircraft flying from RN escorts patrolling in the dangerous northern regions of the gulf proved to be of the greatest value. They were also able to operate away from their mother ship in their search-and-destroy missions by refuelling from ashore or from US vessels.

During hostilities, the Lynx helicopters operated in the enemy's "back yard", and therefore spent a lot of time at high speed and very low level, underneath hostile radar and missile coverage. The enemy air defence system kept the Lynx crews on their toes, and fatigue was a problem for both aircrew and maintenance teams.

On the evening of 29th January, *Cardiff's* helicopter recorded the first Sea Skua success, by destroying an Iraqi gunboat. In the following days, Lynxs ranged the sea areas around the enemy shores, and very quickly cleared them of threatening combatants.

They probed and attacked, operating on their own, or in concert with US helicopters. The growing number of hulks in the area bore witness to the almost total destruction of the Iraqi navy. In general, a single Skua was sufficient to neutralise each target, although some were engaged by two missiles.

When the Allied forces moved en masse to the north on 14th February to establish the amphibious operating area, the Lynxs were employed to defend mine counter measure vessels and other helicopters working in sight of the ene my coast, protecting these vitally important assets from small boat attacks from Kuwait.

In all, Lynxs form HMS *Brazen, Manchester, Cardiff, London* and *Gloucester* fired 26 Sea Skua missiles, of which 22 were direct hits. 12 vessels were destroyed or put out of action.

CONTEMPORARY AIRBORNE OPERATIONS

The decision to use Airborne Forces to spearhead the Allied landings in Normandy in June 1944 was no accident or fluke of military logic. It was based on sound military principles that prevail to this day, in particular, on a clear understanding of the potential of parachute and glider-borne forces to exploit the aerial dimension.

In essence, airborne forces offer military planners two unique capabilities that stand them apart from more conventional formations - reach and responsiveness.

Elements of a four-man pathfinder patrol from 5 Airbourne brigade during a high altitude low opening (HALO) descent. They use GQ360 parachutes and oxygen breathing equipement and are armed with GPMG's and M16A2's.

The UK's 6th Airborne Division and its sister Divisions in the US Army, the 82nd and 101st Airborne Divisions, gave the Allies the ability to gain a foothold in vital areas of the beachhead at a stroke, at night and largely independent of the dispositions of the defenders. In short airborne forces could, in a massive surprise attack, exploit the third, air flank to devastating effect.

The potential utility and importance of Airborne operations remains as great today as it was in 1944. Indeed, the Gulf conflict of 1990/91 perfectly demonstrated the strategic and operational use of air-delivered combat power. Within days of the Iraqi

invasion of Kuwait, in August 1990, the US 82nd Division had, exploiting its light weight, quick response and flexibility, deployed nearly 7,000 miles from its home base in the USA to defensive positions in Saudi Arabia as the first, and, for a while, only element of the Allied Coalition. In this respect the Division demonstrated that airborne forces have become an important political tool, with the potential to take centre stage in the international arena.

Six months later, in February 1991, another veteran of the Normandy battlefield, the US 101st Airborne division gave a stunning display of the exploitation of the third dimension, when it launched itself deep into Iraqi territory to within 60 miles of Baghdad as part of Operation Desert Storm. At a stroke, the 101st's unique capabilities allowed the Coalition to outflank the vast bulk of Saddam Hussein's forces and directly threaten his capital. From the opening moments of the campaign to its dramatic denouement, airborne forces played a key role.

THE UK'S AIRBORNE CAPABILITY TODAY

Today, the UK's airborne force, 5 Airborne Brigade, also stands poised to exploit the third dimension, delivering combat power by air whenever and wherever required, ready to emulate the feats of the airborne divisions both in the Gulf and in Normandy.

Indeed both the roles of the Brigade and the 5,000 men in its ranks bear a remarkable resemblance to those of 6th Airborne Division 50 years ago. Independently, or as part of its parent formation, 3 (UK) Division, the Brigade may be tasked to carry out such classic airborne tasks as:-

● Seize-and-hold operations similar to those mounted on key bridges and terrain features on the night on 5th June 1944;

● Area interdiction operations; and

● Long-range raids.

The Brigade is also trained to conduct Services Protected Evacuations worldwide, operations mounted at the behest of a foreign government and designed to ensure the safe conduct of British and other nationals from any area in which their safety can no longer be guaranteed. In this way the Brigade exploits its unique ability to project combat power over a strategic range and, if necessary, to force an entry into a hostile theatre of operations.

ORGANIZATION

The combat power of 5 Airborne Brigade is built around its two parachute and two airlanded infantry battalions. The leading element for any operation, known as the Leading Parachute Battalion Group (LPBG), is maintained at five days notice to move worldwide and can be inserted over ranges of

A Supacat 6 wheel high mobility load carrying vehicle being driven at speed in very wet conditions.

several thousand nautical miles by RAF C-130 Hercules transport aircraft. This force is an all-arms grouping, complete with specialist pathfinders for the marking of Drop Zones, artillery, air defence systems, light armour, engineers, medical and logistic personnel, all of whom are parachute-trained. The Brigade contains a second parachute Battalion, the Follow Up Parachute Battalion Group (FUPBG) which mirrors the LPBG. The two airlanded infantry battalions specialise in Tactical Airland Landing Operations (TALO) which involve the seizure of airfields in coup de main operations, classically demonstrated by Israeli para commandos during their daring rescue of hostages at Entebbe airport in 1976.

The Brigade is also logistically self contained, a capability provided by another unique airborne formation, the Airborne Logistic Battalion. Finally, but once again demonstrating the truly joint nature of airborne forces, both the RAF and the Army Air Corps provide helicopter support of the Brigade with Lynx, Gazelle, Scout, Puma and Chinook helicopters.

SELECTION

The Airborne soldier himself has changed little over 50

years. He remains a tough, self-disciplined and highly motivated individual, capable, if necessary, of working alone on his own initiative.

All parachute-trained soldiers are volunteers who, before they can gain their coveted Maroon Berets, have been required to complete successfully one of the Army's most rigorous selection courses, P Company. Following a two-week build up, P Company's ten test events are run over a period of seven days and comprise a series of long-distance marches with full equipment over arduous terrain, individual speed events, milling (a form of boxing) and determination, stamina and willpower in its most basic form. Only success on P Company will allow a potential airborne soldier to progress to parachute training.

P Company is designed to take men to what they believe to be their breaking point and then beyond. It aims to prove to them that an indomitable spirit can be made to triumph over any adversity. It

An exhausted officer on the all arms P Company course for Airborne forces selection attempts to climb a hill for the fourth time in succession in unbearably hot weather conditions.

aims to forge the members of the Brigade into one cohesive whole, building bonds of mutual trust and respect between its disparate members. In short, P Company is vital to the building of the Airborne ethos, the will to succeed in the face of every setback, against the toughest of opposition and with the most limited of material means.

In addition our airland infantry battalions are now required to complete an Airborne Inductions (ABI) Package, another physically demanding course designed to introduce them to the rigours of service with the Brigade.

The outstanding individual qualities fostered by courses such as P Company and the resultant indomitable camaraderie were amply demonstrated in 1944. Such qualities were, once again, brought to the fore when, during the 1982 Falklands conflict, two of our Parachute Battalions and our Gurkha Battalion were required to fight and

defeat a numerically superior and well-prepared enemy over 8,000 miles from the UK home-base and in the most appalling climatic conditions.

FUTURE DEVELOPMENTS

Today, 5 Airborne Brigade is a force which embodies strategic reach, rapid responses and considerable combat power. But against the backdrop of a changing international political scene, it continues to evolve to face today's unique challenges.

Whilst the bedrock of the Brigade, its ethos, remains preserved and fostered by rigorous selection, its tactical techniques and equipment are under constant review. The Brigade is currently refining its parachuting techniques as a result of the development of a UK-manufactured low level parachute (LLP). This system will give the Brigade a world-wide leading ability to drop from heights as low as 250 feet, greatly increasing the survivability of the C-130 force in a hostile air defence environment.

Further developments in platform delivery systems are aimed at mirroring this new drop height and at increasing the weight of stores delivered by parachute. At the same time, developments in avionics, such as the Global Positioning System satellite navigation aid, will increase the Brigade's ability to drop with pin-point accuracy in zero visibility. Finally, the fielding of new equipment such as the Army Air

Corp's Attack Helicopter will see a quantum leap in combat power that can be delivered from the air.

The exploitation of the third flank remains as potentially exciting and promising in military terms now as it was 50 years ago. In 5 Airborne Brigade, the men who seized the Merville battery and Pegasus Bridge have worthy successors. Those men know that to remain a force for all seasons today's airborne soldiers must remain as they always have been - ad unum omnes...

... *ALL TO ONE PURPOSE!*

ROYAL AIR FORCE - SUPPORT HELICOPTER FORCE

The Royal Air Force operates three types of support helicopter. The heavy lift capability is provided by the Chinook HCI, of which there is one squadron, No 7, at RAF Odiham. There is also a composite squadron of Chinooks and Pumas serving with No 2 Group in Germany at RAF Laarbruch. Two further Puma squadrons are based in the UK, No 33 at Odiham, and No 230 at RAF Aldergrove in Ulster. Training on the Chinook and Puma is carried out at No 240 Operational Conversion Unit, also at Odiham. The third type is the Wessex, which equips No 72 Squadron at Aldergrove, and No 60 Squadron at RAF Benson in Oxfordshire.

The Chinook is a twin-engined, twin-rotor aircraft made by Boeing-Vertol. At a cruising speed of around 140kts it has a

range of over 600 miles, can lift a payload of over 27,000 lbs and usually carries up to 44 fully-equipped troops. However, in the Falklands conflict, the sole survivor of the sinking of the Atlantic Conveyor carried 88, all standing. It has a triple-hook external cargo system, of which the centre suspension system is rated at 12,700 lbs. The aircraft first entered service with No 240 OCU at the end of 1980, and the fleet is now undergoing a major update and refurbishment programme at the manufacturers.

The Puma was an Aerospatiale design and the French built pre-production aircraft was used as a pattern aircraft for the British production batch, which were built by Westland. The aircraft first entered service with the Royal Air Force in 1971. It has twin Tubomeca turbine engines of 1,328 shp and these give the aircraft the ability to carry a maximum load of 7,000 lbs. It cruises at 130 kts over a range of 300 nautical miles and has space for up to 20 troops.

The Wessex in RAF service is powered by two 1,550 shp Rolls-Royce Gnome coupled shaft turbines. It can carry a maximum load of 3,000 lbs underslung and there is fuselage capacity for 16 troops. It first entered service with the Royal Air Force at Odiham in 1964. The last Wessex to be built were used to equip the Queen's Flight at RAF Benson in 1969. Thus this durable aircraft achieves 30 years in RAF front-line service this year.

During the Gulf War both Pumas and Chinooks were deployed to the Arabian peninsula as part of a joint Support

Above
RAF Chinooks of 24 Air Mobile brigade take off after off-loading troops.

Left
An RAF Puma helicopter operating in Norway in the logistic support role.

Helicopter Force. Directly tasked by the Corps ASOC, they were an integral part of the support for the clandestine move by the armoured brigades to their more westerly start positions, and then during the dramatic advance through southern Iraq to the Basra road.

Immediately after the defeat of Saddam, the plight of the Kurds drew international support. In the aftermath of the war, No 240 OCU provided the initial Chinook element of the force. The first three aircraft began their 20-hour, three-day self-ferry to theatre on 11th April 1991 and the first two arrived at Incerlik in Turkey on 13th April 1991 with the third a day later.

The aircraft were tasked on the day after their arrival to go to the far east of the country to a Turkish base in the mountains called Hakkari, to set up operations in support of the Turkish authorities. The distance between Hakkari and Incerlik, 350 miles, meant that the RAF Chinooks, which had been fitted with long-range fuel tanks for the deployment, were the only helicopters with sufficient range to operate in support of the Hakkari detachment. The Kurds were dying of dehydration and starvation, and for two weeks aid had been limited to airdrops, which were unable to reach the refugee sites on the mountain ridges. The crews found themselves flying into camps where no previous aid had been provided, and these early sorties proved to be the most harrowing, even for the most hardened of crews.

The people were so desperate that young mothers would throw their infants onto the ramps of the Chinooks in the belief that anywhere would be better than awful conditions in the camps. As the scale of the problem in the mountains became clear, the size of the detachment was increased to ten aircraft with the additional airframes being taken from a ship diverted on its return journey from the Gulf. At the same time the main mounting base was moved to the Turkish fighter base at Diyabakir with a Forward Operating base at Silopi. Over the first three weeks of the operation, the RAF Chinooks flew 645 hours, carried 1,300 tons of relief stores and moved 800 refugees, of whom 253 were evacuated to field hospitals.

As the mountains of Eastern Turkey rise to 13,500 ft, and temperatures at low level could be as high as 50 degrees centigrade the aircraft were not knowingly operated at weights above 19,000 kg. Subsequently four Chinooks of the detachment were placed under the command of 3 Commando Brigade to provide additional lift, particularly in hot and high conditions. This assisted the rapid establishment of the safe havens for the Kurdish people.

Subsequently, back in Europe, the support helicopter force has continued to support the Army in Ulster. These operations involved all three types. Simultaneously the force has provided support for major exercises involving 24 Airmobile Brigade, the Multi-National Northag Airmobile Division and the Allied Command Europe Mobile Force.

For many years the RAF support helicopter squadrons have been the most heavily committed of the service's flying units. A testimony to the utility and flexibility of the force.

THE HERCULES FORCE

The Lockheed C130 Hercules has been the mainstay of the Royal Air Force transport force since the end of the 1960s. The first aircraft entered service at RAF Thorney Island on 3 May 1967, but since the 1975 defence reorganisation, all the Hercules transport force has been based at RAF Lyneham in Wiltshire, where the aircraft equips Nos 24, 30, 47, and 70 Squadrons and the Hercules OCU No 57 (Reserve) Squadron.

There are basically two models of the Hercules in RAF service. Both are powered by four Allison turboprop engines which give the aircraft a maximum payload of just over 400,000 lbs, and a range of about 3,000 nautical miles, with a cruising speed of 315 kts. The difference between the CMk1 and CMk3 is the length of the hold. In 1980 a number of the original CMk1s were converted by adding an extra 15 ft to the fuselage. This has increased the maximum load volume from: 92 to 126 passengers, 64 to 90 paratroopers, or five to seven pallets.

In the tactical support role the aircraft can make a medium-level transit using station-keeping radar to maintain formation and then approach the drop-zone, or airhead, at low-level to drop, or airland, troops and equipment. Night Vision Goggles give the capability to carry out unlit operations including airfield assault. A small number of the force have been converted to a tactical air refuelling configuration, and there is a single "weather laboratory" version operated by the Meteorological Research Flight at RAF Farnborough.

While not involved in the parachute role during the Gulf War, the Hercules played a very full part. Indeed, the first Hercules left Lyneham less than 24 hours after the operation was mounted. During the long build-up to the actual conflict the Hercules fleet and RAF Lyneham sustained phenomenal work and tasking schedules. Over 40,000 hours were flown in the first seven months, more than twice the normal rate. While the bulk of the flying was concerned with the strategic deployment of the operational squadrons, and the armoured brigades, to the Arabian Peninsular, some tactical support sorties were flown in theatre delivering supplies to, and airlifting casualties from, forward sites.

Immediately after the end of the Gulf War, the plight of Kurdish refugees prompted airdrops in the harsh mountainous terrain of the Iraq/Turkey border. In a four-week period of very testing flying, three aircraft operating out of Incerlik dropped over 1,000,000 lbs of relief supplies.

Subsequently the Hercules forces moved the support equipment and vehicles required by 3 Royal Marine Commando in their duties protecting the Kurds in the safe-haven camps. The Hercules flew into Diyabakir in Turkey and to Sirsenk in Iraq itself. In the three years since these operations the Hercules have been involved in further humanitarian operations in the former Yugoslavia, and Somalia, as well as maintaining the re-supply of the RAF contingents still deployed in support of the persecuted minorities in Iraq. In peace, as in war, the range, load-carrying, airdrop and rough-strip capabilities of the Hercules mean that it is always in demand.

Left
*The crew
of an RAF
C130 Hercules
look warily through
the starboard cockpit windows
as their plane banks hard whilst flying
at under 85 metres during the run-in to the drop zone.*

*A close-up
view of the nose of
an RAF C130 Hercules in flight.*

THE ROYAL MARINE COMMANDOS

The Royal Marines of the 1990s continue to provide Sea Soldiers for our maritime nation.

This service can be traced back to 1664 when the forebears of the Royal Marines, the "Admiral's Regiment", was raised.

It was in World War Two that the first Royal Marine Commandos were formed from the RM Division and the Mobile Naval Defence Organisation - 40 Commando rebuilt itself from the survivors of Dieppe while the 8thBattalion became 41 Commando.

In 1943 the Commando Training School in Achnacarry turned out 42, 43, 44, 45, 46, 47 and 48 Commandos.

The Commando function was shared with the Army until 1946 when the Royal Marines took over the role.

For more than 20 years after World War Two, the Royal Marines were engaged in almost continuous active service, including the Korean War and campaigns in Palestine (1946-48), Malaya (1950-52), Cyprus (1954-56), Suez (1956), Aden and Southern Arabia (1960-67), Brunei (1962), Borneo (1962-66), and East Africa (1964).

After the withdrawal of a military presence from most overseas bases in the 60s and 70s, government policy led to a new and demanding role for the Royal Marines within NATO, culminating in 1979 with the whole of 3 Commando Brigade being committed to Arctic warfare, but retaining the capability of world-wide deployment and taking their turn with army units for operational tours principally in Northern Ireland, Belize and with the United Nations.

When the Argentineans invaded the Falkland Islands, 3 Commando Brigade was immediately despatched to the South Atlantic and played a major part in the recapture of the Islands. It was the perfect scenario for Royal Marines Commandos, with an amphibious assault, a rugged approach march and a tough final battle in adverse conditions of both weather and terrain. Royal Marines were engaged in all phases of the Campaign. They served as detachments in many HM Ships, as coxswains

Royal Marines pose around Government House after re-capturing Port Stanley during the 1982 Falklands War.

Royal Marine Commando's patrol past Kurdish Guerilla fighters during the UN mandated Humanitarian relief operation in Kurdistan in 1991.

Royal Marine Commandos dressed in Arctic Warfare clothing on exercise in Norway. The ability of the Royal Marine Commandos to operate in such extreme conditions is a reflection of their unique capability to undertake difficult tasks.

of landing craft, as commandos on the ground, helicopter pilots and in the Royal Marines Special Forces unit - The Special Boat Service.

The 1990s are providing new challenges, demonstrated by 3 Commando Brigade spearheading the deployment into Northern Iraq to provide protection and humanitarian assistance to the Kurdish refugees.

The dramatic events that have transformed the European and global security environment over the past few years have placed even more emphasis on the requirement for a flexible and mobile amphibious force that can offer the unique combination of strategic reach and operational mobility. Within the context of the National Defence Policy unveiled in 1992, the Government remains firmly committed to a national amphibious capability.

No. 3 Commando Brigade Royal Marines is the operational (land) formation which carries out amphibious operations. In

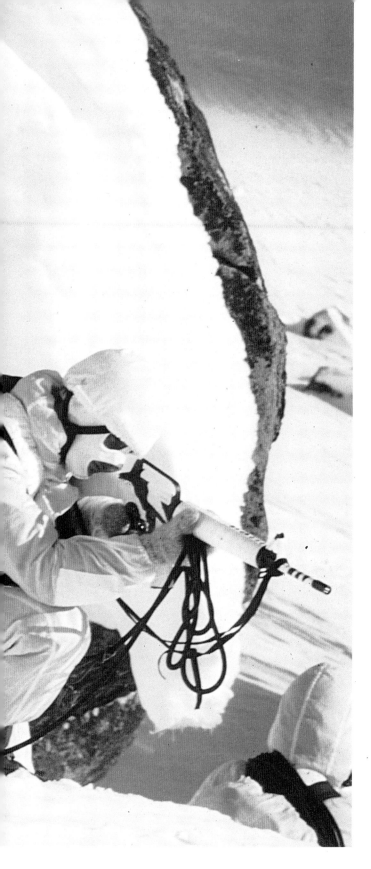

Units: 40, 42 and 45 Commandos. These units contain 658 men, and are capable of operating in extreme environments any where in the world including, mountain and cold weather, jungle and desert environments. The versatility of the Commando units and the quality of their training are illustrated by their crucial role in the Falklands conflict in 1982 and Northern Iraq in 1990.

In addition, Commando Units have undertaken over 30 tours in Northern Ireland, plus numerous other operations around the world.

As well as rifles and bayonets, a Commando's modern arsenal contains MILAN anti-tank guided missiles, 81mm Mortars, medium machine-guns and light anti-tank weapons.

● Indirect fire support is provided by 29 Commando Regiment Royal Artillery, which has three regular and one Territorial Army (TA) batteries equipped with 105mm Light Guns, and an additional battery that is trained and equipped to direct naval gunfire from Royal Navy ships in support of land operations. The Royal Artillery also provides an Air Defence Battery.

● Integral air support is provided by 3 Commando Brigade Air Squadron, which is equipped with Lynx and Gazelle helicopters. Support helicopters, Sea King mark 4, are furnished by Naval Air Squadrons.

● The Commando Logistic Regiment is responsible for providing the Brigade with all its integral logistic and medical support.

● Engineer expertise is provided by one regular and one TA engineer squadron - 59 and 131 Independent Commando Squadrons Royal Engineers.

● A Headquarters and Signal Squadron furnishes the Brigade Commander with communications; point air defence, tactical air control parties and a Brigade Patrol Troop which provides the Brigade Commander with his reconnaissance capability. This small but potent force is trained and equipped to provide early warning and intelligence up to 60 kilometres ahead of the main body of the Brigade.

● Meanwhile 539 Assault Squadron Royal Marines provides integral amphibious support. It is equipped with a variety of craft that are designed for amphibious landings, raids and re-supply.

● The Brigade will also be supported by the Royal Marines Special Forces - the Special Boat Service. Its roles include beach reconnaissance, observation, attacks on enemy shipping and other offensive actions of the type for which the 'Cockleshell Heroes' are famous.

As well as specialist personnel, amphibious operations require specialist ships. The inventory consists of five Landing Ships Logistic (LSLs) and two Landing Platform Docks (LPDs), HMS Fearless and HMS Intrepid. The LPDs have a flight deck, dock and crucial command and control facilities. They can carry heavy equipment and 300 to 400 troops (numbers will depend on length of passage and area of operation). In addition, a helicopter carrier, HMS Ocean has

the context of NATO, the Brigade, together with elements of the Royal Netherlands Marine Corps, make up the United Kingdom/Netherlands Landing Force - the only fully integrated bi-national brigade in NATO. This formation provides a useful political and strategic tool. The RNLMC contribution includes a marine battalion, a 120mm mortar battery, logistic support and landing craft. The Brigade is constituted from a cross section of specialist units.

● The cutting edge is provided by the three Commando

been ordered. This ship will replace an important capability that was lost when HMS *Hermes* was disposed of in 1984.

The Royal Marines are particularly skilled in working with helicopters, having been involved in such operations since their inception at Suez in 1956. A helicopter assault is now a basic component of contemporary amphibious operations.

Meanwhile, Royal Marines continue to serve in a number of HM Ships, land-based detachments and training teams, and as part of many UN operations. Comacchio Group protects Britain's independent nuclear deterrent and undertakes other naval security tasks.

All Royal Marines have to undergo and pass the rugged Commando Course, at the end of which they are entitled to wear the coveted Green Beret. But this is only at the end of eight months training. For the greater part of this time the recruit will be based at the Commando Training Centre at Lympstone, near Exmouth, where he will learn a wide range of commando skills that complement the rigorous physical training.

There is an emphasis on individual and team skills as well as extensive weapon training and tactical instruction. The Commando test, all of which must be conducted in "combat fighting order" with weapons, starts in the 28th week: the Tarzan and Assault Course is conducted over a series of confidence-building obstacles below, on and above the ground; The Endurance Course involves negotiating one-and-a-half miles of rough terrain, including water obstacles, deep culverts, pools and bogs, followed by a four-mile run and culminating with a live firing test.

The Nine-Mile Speed March is to be completed in 90 minutes followed by a troop attack. A 30ft rope climb in full kit and a battle swimming test must also be passed. The final test is to complete 30 miles across Dartmoor in eight hours. Officers undertake the same tests as the recruits although faster timings must be achieved. Officer training takes two years, 15 months at the Commando Training Centre and nine months with an operational unit.

Although the weapons, uniform and craft of today's Royal Marines Commandos are somewhat different to those of the 17,500 Royal Marines that took part in the D-Day landings, the Commando spirit survives and is at the very root of today's Corps.

The new world order has led to an increased need for mobile and flexible amphibious forces.

The utility of today's Royal Marines is demonstrated by the range of operations to which they contribute – from humanitarian relief to high-intensity conflict, performing military functions at the strategic, operational and tactical levels of war.

These forces are included in all Defence Roles outlined by the Government, they can act independently, within a NATO Multinational Maritime Force, as part of the ACE Rapid Reaction Corps or as an element within a wider coalition operation built around the Western European Union or UN.

LANDING CRAFT OPERATIONS

Several different types of landing and raiding craft are operated by Royal Marines today to meet a variety of roles. The most traditional role is to man the Landing Craft Utility (LCU) and the Landing Craft Vehicle Personnel (LCVP) from the Landing Platform Docks (LPDs). The LCU Mk 9 is a 100-ton displacement craft designed to carry heavy loads of vehicles and stores, and four of which operate from the dock of the LPD.

The coxswain is a Senior NCO and the total crew is seven men. The LCU can also carry 120 men and is now fitted with a fibreglass canopy. Although it has a relatively slow speed of nine knots, it has a good range of 600 nautical miles.

The LCVP is crewed by a Corporal and two Marines, and the LPD operates four of these Craft from its davits. They are primarily assault craft and have a good speed and range, and they too have canopies. They are designed to carry a rifle troop.

Additionally, 539 Assault Squadron RM also operates LCVPs and LCUs but has significant differences from the assault squadrons in the LPD. It was created and equipped with 16 Rigid Raiding Craft (RRC). The new RRC Mk 2 is driven by a Marine coxswain, has a speed in excess of 25 knots and is designed to carry a rifle section of eight men with all their equipment.

All the craft mentioned so far offer enormous flexibility to the commander of an amphibious landing force for landing or assault operations, but may also be used for raiding, and subsequently to redeploy Marines or operate along coasts or shorelines. In particular, 539 Assault Squadron specialises in raiding techniques, and also operates from shore or island bases.

This Squadron also now operates four Hovercraft which are crewed by a corporal and a marine, both landing craft specialists; powered by a diesel engine and designed to carry 16 fully-equipped troops; these craft give tremendous scope and flexibility for fast operations in excess of 30 knots without the need to search for suitable beaches required by conventional craft.

Landing craft-qualified Marines also operate high speed Rigid Inflatable Boats with various units. Because they do not need to be beached these craft have more seaworthy and capable hulls than the RRC but require very special techniques. They are used to provide security and customs patrols in Diego Garcia, Scotland and Northern Ireland, and perhaps the most challenging task is in Hong Kong: here extremely fast craft are required to be launched from the Hong Kong Patrol Ships, capable of intercepting, challenging, and boarding high-speed boats being used for smuggling.

The additional role of Royal Marines manning landing craft and small boats is even more relevant than in the past: modern warfare requires high-speed craft, and advanced technology, which demand high professional standards coupled with traditional seamanship skills.

*T*he people of Portsmouth salute with affection, pride and gratitude all who took part in the D-Day operation. We remember those who died, those who returned, and those 'at home' who provided such valiant support.

We are indebted to their bravery and courage. Out of their sacrifice comes our freedom.

Portsmouth
City Council

CONTEMPORARY ROYAL ENGINEERS

Today, the Corps of Royal Engineers comprises some 20 regiments totalling more than 14,000 personnel, just over half of which are in the Regular Army, with the balance found from their Territorial counterparts. The combat engineer skills in mobility, countermobility and survivability remain of considerable importance but more recently there has been a shift in emphasis towards more generic engineer support in which construction engineering and artisan skills are assuming greater prominence.

As ever, flexibility is the key word and the Sapper of today must be able to turn his hand quickly and effectively to any of his skills.

COMBAT SKILLS

Taking the combat engineer dimension first, mobility support remains a fundamental task. The demands of mechanised warfare are such that obstacles such as rivers or minefields must be able to be crossed with the minimum of delay. In the forward combat areas this requires engineer tanks equipped with a variety of bridging equipment. This will include the

No 10 Close Support Bridge being launched by Chieftain Bridgelayer. A 23m bridge can be put in place in about five minutes.

168

Chieftain mounted components of the new Bridging for the 90s system about to enter service.

For shorter gaps fascines are still used, albeit in a more modern form. These are carried on a further Chieftain variant, the AVRE. The top hamper carries three pipe fascines, five rolls of MLC70 trackway or general engineer stores. The AVRE can operate a dozer blade for digging tank scrapes for gun emplacements, mineplough for clearing minefields, Giant Viper - an explosive minefield clearance system, and can tow Barminelayer behind an AVRE trailer. It is fitted with a crane giving it a self-loading capability and has a four-man crew.

Where bridging operations can be conducted without the threat of enemy direct fire weapons, armoured vehicles are less important. The new wheeled Bridging for the 90s equipment will form the majority of our general support bridging. A typical 32m bridge can be built by ten men in less than 30 minutes.

For wider rivers more sophisticated equipment is available. The amphibious M2 can be used either as a ferry or as a bridge. Its replacement, M3, offers greater carrying capacity and speed of operation and will enter service shortly.

Man-made obstacles, primarily minefields, continue to present a significant problem. Hand breaching is now too slow and more advanced techniques have been developed. Explosive clearance devices and plough tanks are essential. The Royal Engineers have Giant Viper and the plough fitted to the AVRE to provide this capability.

Countermobility too retains its significance although, to match developments in doctrine, the emphasis is less on creating major obstacle belts and more on the rapid creation of obstacles to match the developing tactical situation. Scatterable mines are now entering service as are much more rapid demolition techniques.

The Engineer contribution to survivability covers a vast range of activities. The traditional fortifications remain vital and the Combat Engineer Tractor plays an important role as an armoured digging machine and amphibious pathfinder.

Explosive Ordnance Disposal is particularly important in the rear areas where the logistic resupply of the forward brigades can be greatly disrupted by unexploded munitions and mines. Royal Engineer bomb disposal officers are trained to deal with modern battlefield munitions as well as ordnance dating back to WWII and before.

The last combat-related area covers support to the Royal Air Force. Royal Engineers support RAF operations from both conventional airfields used by fixed wing aircraft such as Tornado, and temporary improvised flying sites used by Harrier. The versatile Harrier can operate from very short strips, either constructed by the Royal Engineers using a light alloy matting, or modified existing road surfaces. The Royal Engineers also construct tactical hides from modified existing buildings.

The repair of more conventional airfield facilities in war, including rapid runway repair and the maintenance of essential

facilities such as electricity and water on the airfield, falls to the Royal Engineers. Airfield Damage Repair troops can make a temporary repair to a concrete operating surface capable of taking fast jets in a few hours. Teams of artisan tradesmen can repair electricity cables and water pipes in a similar time frame to keep the airfield operational following an enemy attack.

CONSTRUCTION SKILLS

In many operations short of war, such as Bosnia, or in peace support operations, it is the construction side of the Royal Engineers that assumes prominence. The need is to help the Army to live and move and this involves the construction of roads and camps, and the provision of essential services (power, water, fuel and drainage). The Corps retains the skills required to carry out reconnaissance, planning and design, as well as construction on site.

The provisions of roads, water and fuel are of particular significance once modern infrastructure has collapsed and this too falls to the Royal Engineers.

Chieftain AVRE with Pipe Fascines and a Trailer with MLC70 trackway

THE ROYAL ARMOURED CORPS

The recent announcement that the Royal Armoured Corps is to have a new fleet of tanks has confirmed the importance that the Army attaches to its Armoured regiments. In spite of cuts to the British Army, which will leave the Corps with 44 per cent fewer soldiers than in 1990, the effectiveness of the fighting units will remain as strong as it was on the 6th June 1944.

The Corps today has two types of regiment. First, eight Regiments in the armoured role equipped with Main Battle Tanks, Challenger which served so well during the liberation of Kuwait and Chieftain which has been in service since the 1960s.

The role of these regiments is to provide the battlefield commander with his main strike force; and their primary task is to defeat the enemy by using heavy firepower in conjunction with good mobility.

When the new tank, Challenger 2, comes into service next year the armoured regiments will possess one of the deadliest fighting platforms in the world.

Second, there are two regiments of Light Armour which are normally deployed in the reconnaissance role but, because of their flexibility, they can be used for other tasks as seen in the continuing presence of the Light Dragoons in Bosnia.

They have vehicles which are small, fast and armed with the accurate 30mm cannon which can fire six rounds in less

than five seconds. They will normally operate ahead of the main force obtaining and reporting information which is critical to the commanders plan.

The amalgamation of regiments over the last two years has seen the disappearance of the great names associated with the D-Day landings. However, the Royal Armoured Corps has come out of this difficult period with new regiments dedicated to upholding the history and traditions created by their predecessors.

THE YEOMANRY

The Yeomanry is a vital element of the Reserve Army. There are now five

Royal Armoured Corps Tank Regiments are currently equipped with the Challenger Mark 2 main battle tank. The Challenger Mark 1 distinguished itself in action during the Gulf war outgunning and outranging the Iraqi opposition.

173

regiments and an independent squadron each supporting one of the Army's districts.

The Queens Own Yeomanry, based in the North of England, are converting to armoured reconnaissance and will become the Rapid Reaction Corps' dedicated reconnaissance regiment. They are giving up their Fox armoured vehicles for the more effective tracked Scimitar. Their role will be identical to that of a regular regiment with a primary task of operating ahead of the main force gathering information which is vital to the battlefield commander's plan. As the soldiers will be trained in armoured reconnaissance skills they could be called up at short notice to reinforce the regular regiments in times of war.

The other four regiments (Royal, Royal Wessex, Royal Mercian and Lancastrian and Scottish) and the independent squadron (North Irish House) are all National Defence Yeomanry and are equipped with Land-Rovers. They are the Army's light reconnaissance forces who, due to their flexibility, can be used in a variety of roles ranging from reconnaissance of the battlefield in times of war to guarding key installations in the UK. They could also be called up to provide individual reinforcement for the regular Army as they have many of the skills required to fight alongside their regular counterparts.

During the Cold War years, The Queens Own Yeomanry and the Royal Yeomanry were roled to 1 (BR) Corps in Germany mounted in Saladin and Ferrets and latterly Fox armoured Cars, and the others in the Home Defence role in Land-Rovers.

Now, as a result of Options For Change The Queens Own

Armoured Reconaissance regiments in the regular army and some Yeomanry regiments in the territorial army are equipped with the Scimitar armed reconaissance vehicle, here shown at speed in desert conditions.

Yeomanry is assigned to the Allied Rapid Reaction Corps Recce Branch being re-equipped with Scimitar, while the rest are in the National Defence Role in Land-Rovers.

Despite all the amalgamations and role-changes the Yeomanry still takes immense pride in its county connections, they are the unbreakable umbilical cord that keeps its spirit alive and as a result the connections with local communities are as strong as ever.

The importance of territorial links are as strong to the Yeomanry as they were to its forebears'. Up against the background of a society which sometimes questions the relevance of the Forces, until times of crisis, a society with a non-military ethos since 1945; a society driven by a professional rather than a voluntary ethos, it is astounding that the Yeomanry is able to recruit large numbers of men and women of the high-

est quality, the majority of whom are leading a full family and working life, but who still volunteer for the Yeomanry.

The TA is sometimes referred to as the 'Army of the Unemployed' - this is an insult to those families who give up so much. The Queens Own Yeomanry recruits from Merseyside, Tyneside, Yorkshire and Nottinghamshire and the unemployed amongst its ranks is under 15 per cent.

The quality of its soldiers has never been higher nor their dedication to duty surpassed, the professionalism that is expected of them has never been greater, its wives and families never so supportive, and the customary enthusiasm of the Yeoman has never been better. However 'the spirit of the volunteer' is a tenuous thing and can never be taken for granted.

The Yeomanry's young soldiers join for many and varied reasons. They should be supported in order to see the continuance of a great British institution.

The Yeomanry Cavalry dates from 1794. It was the first properly established, part-time, volunteer mounted force raised for the defence of the realm, and it has been in continuous existence ever since.

For the first 100 years of its history, the purpose of the Yeomanry was for home defence, which included giving aid to the civil power in times of disorder. By the 1870s, that role, happily was a matter of the past and, depending on wars and rumours of wars, the Yeomanry Cavalry continued to train for the defence of the country.

As the most prestigious of the volunteer military organisations, the social composition of the Yeomanry Cavalry changed little over the years. The commissioned ranks were filled by local land-owners and the well-to-do. The yeoman themselves were mainly farmers, men connected with the land or of some standing in the towns.

They had to provide their own horses and contributed from their own purse for membership. They formed themselves into troops according to locality and gradually developed the squadron, regimental and brigade organisation which we would more or less recognise in modern times.

And this year all the Yeomanry Regiments will parade in Windsor Great Park for a Royal Review in the presence of Her Majesty The Queen in order to celebrate 200 years of Yeoman Service

THE ROYAL ARTILLERY TODAY

Since 1945 the Royal Artillery has fought in many low intensity operations around the world - often as infantry - but Korea, the Falklands and the Gulf bore some relationship to their operations on D-Day. Since all military operations are some combination of 'Fire and Movement', the role of the Royal Artillery as one of the key combat arms is still to find the enemy and then to destroy him by firepower.

The latest self propelled gun to enter British army service is the AS90. Here it fires its main 150mm armament on Larkhill artillery ranges.

To do this the Royal Artillery is divided into the two categories of 'surface-to-surface' and 'surface-to-air' artillery. But the whole organization is today very small although the capability of its weapons is very great. Until 1992 all nuclear weapons in the Army were in the Royal Artillery but these, since the end of the Cold War, no longer exist.

The surface-to-surface artillery consists of:-

• Firstly five regiments of armoured artillery each of four eight-gun batteries of the new AS 90 gun (32 guns in a regiment) and a headquarters battery equipped with mortar and locating radars. These are, 1st and 3rd Regiments Royal Horse Artillery (RHA) 4th, 26th and 40th Regiments. The AS 90 has a range in excess of 30,000 yards and has a burst fire capability of three rounds in ten seconds. It can come into a position and survey itself in and be ready in seconds. Fire control is by computer and permits the Forward Observation Officer (FOO) using a laser range finder, to pass firing data through a computer in the command post direct to the gun sights. The new 155mm shell fuse is very powerful and destructive.

• Secondly three regiments of light guns each also of four batteries of eight 105mm light guns (32 in a regiment) and a headquarters battery also equipped with mortar locating radars. These are 7th Parachute Regiment RHA, 19th Airmobile Regiment and 29th Commando Regiment. The light gun has a range of 19,000 yards and can be air dropped, sea landed as it was in the Falklands or carried by helicopter. These regiments also use the computer fire control system.

● Thirdly three heavy regiments of rocket artillery each of two rocket batteries of nine launchers (18 in a regiment). Two, 32nd and 39th Regiments, have a locating battery which includes a remotely-piloted aircraft to locate enemy at long range and the third, 5th Regiment, has a special OP battery instead. All have a headquarters battery. The Multi Launch Rocket System (MLRS) has a range in excess of 30,000 yards and was used to devastating effect in the Gulf War. These regiments also use the computer fire control system.

Surface-to-air artillery consists of:-

● Firstly, two regiments of medium air defence artillery each of three batteries of Rapier air defence missiles and a headquarters battery. Rapier has an all-weather, 24-hour capability up to 10,000 feet and is deadly accurate. It is controlled from divisional headquarters by the Air Defence Command and Information System (ADCIS) to ensure reliable links with the RAF. They are, 16th and 22nd Regiments, the latter unit has an extra commando battery.

● Secondly, two regiments of close air defence artillery each of three batteries of 36 Starstreak High Velocity Missiles (HVM) launchers. HVM is a laser-controlled system with a range of some 5,000 feet and is deadly against low flying fixed wing aircraft and helicopters. It is also controlled by ADCIS. They are, 12th and 47th Regiments.

Then there is the artillery of the Allied Mobile force which consists of the British Force Artillery Headquarters and 19/5th Light Battery of six 105mm light guns and a headquarters battery. There are in addition light batteries from five other NATO countries.

THE TERRITORIAL ARMY

The Gunners of the Territorial Army (TA) consist of the same two categories and are very much part of the Army as a whole.

● Firstly, two regiments of field artillery each of three six-gun batteries of FH 70 155mm guns. They are designed to reinforce the artillery of the two divisions in the Army today. They are 100th and 101st Regiments.

● Secondly, three regiments of close air defence artillery each of three batteries of 12 Starburst laser guided command line of sight, shoulder-launched missiles. They are designed to reinforce the air defence capability of the Allied Rapid Reaction Corps (ARRC) in war.

● Thirdly ,but by no means last, considering its ancient traditions, is the Honourable Artillery Company which has a special observation role in the ARRC and is organised into three sabre squadrons.

TRAINING AND HEADQUARTERS

All specialist training is carried out at the Royal School of Artillery at Larkhill. There is a missile-firing range in the Outer Hebrides and at Manorbier in South Wales. There are artillery headquarters at HQ UK Land Forces, at the HQ ARRC in Germany, at HQ 1st Armoured Division also in Germany and at HQ 3rd Mechanised Division in UK. Recruits receive their basic training at Pirbright and their specialist training at Larkhill.

REGIMENTAL ISSUES

The Regimental Headquarters is still at Woolwich, the home of the Royal Artillery for almost 300 years. It is now reduced to the RA Band Woolwich but this is a State band and remains a full orchestra as well. The RA Institution, the RA Association, the RA Charitable Fund and the RA Historical Affairs Committee are all based at Woolwich. The total unit is run as one large Regiment composed of 22 regular and TA family regiments each with their own recruiting areas and hierarchy. Men seldom change regiments but can, in the interests of the Army or for career reasons. Recruiting is good. Today six regiments are stationed in Germany and the rest in the UK. At any one time there will probably be one regiment in Cyprus on UN peacekeeping duties and one or two operating in Northern Ireland as infantry. Many serve all over the world on UN or special duties, as advisors and instructors.

The Regiment has now decided to build a new National Museum of Artillery in some splendid listed buildings which have just become available in the Royal Arsenal by the Thames at Woolwich. They are in excellent condition and one is the very building where the Regiment was formed in 1716. It is planned to create a state of the art, yet dignified display to act as a memorial to all Gunners of the Commonwealth who died in the service of the guns. It will tell the story of artillery in the British Army from its first appearance at Crecy in 1346 to the present day and a major display will certainly cover the action of the guns on D-Day and beyond. The Regiment has already raised £2 million of the £10 million it needs and the Master Gunner is asking all Gunners everywhere to do all they can to ensure that this important and worthwhile project succeeds.

(Details from, The Museum Project Office, Front Parade, RA Barracks, Woolwich , London SE18 4BH).

A javelin air defence missile is launched by a two-man team from 7 Para Royal Horse Artillery during a training exercise in Norway.

KUWAIT: AN HISTORICAL OUTLINE

Kuwait has long been the site of an urban community as it has enjoyed the position of both a land and maritime link to different parts of the old world. Kathima was a station for caravans coming from Persia and Mesopotamia bound for the eastern and central Arabian Peninsula. Failaka Island was a station for commercial fleets, as were other ports from the cape of the Arabian Gulf towards the southern parts enroute to Oman, India, and East Africa.

Historians have not pinpointed Kuwait's origin but have associated it to the influxation of al-Utub tribe in the late seventeenth century, which formed the nucleus of the Kuwaiti community with its prominent ruling family, al-Sabah. By the beginning of the eighteenth century these tribes had been transformed to an urban society with a clear political identity. Historic data which supports Kuwait's early identity includes the observations of Murtada bin Elwan, a traveller who visited Kuwait in 1709, and described it as enjoying a distinguished urban status, and the documents of the British archives, which indicate that the first al-Sabah ruler was governing in 1716. In addition, the Kuwaiti community has long had distinctive borders separating it from the Ottoman Empire and its other neighbours. Several cartographic works and travellers' logs of the eighteenth and nineteenth centuries specify these borders as do many international political documents. (*)

When Iraq and countries of the Levant gained their independence from Turkish influence in the early twentieth century, the newly formed countries were eager to identify and promulgate their borders. Iraq exchanged memoranda with Kuwait regarding this issue which led to the mutual recognition of the existing borders between the two countries; these memoranda were deposited in the United Nations' files. The borders were reconfirmed in a later treaty between the Amir of Kuwait and the Prime Minister of Iraq on October 4, 1963. These borders are the same that the United Nations Demarcation Committee identified as a result of its research which commenced after the liberation of Kuwait in February, 1991, and culminated in its Decree 833 of May, 27, 1993. session 3224. The Committee identified borders according to their findings, neither expanding Kuwait's land at the expense of Iraq's nor denying Iraq access to the Arabian Gulf.

As Kuwait enters the twenty-first century, its identity as an independent, sovereign state is unquestionable. The voices of time have strengthened this final chorus of liberty.

(*) See: *Kuwait-Iraq Boundary Demarcation,* Center for Research and Studies on Kuwait, 1994.

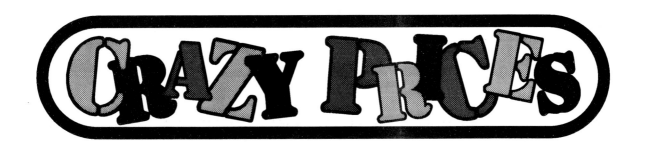

STEWARTS AND CRAZY PRICES

SUPERMARKETS

NORTHERN IRELAND

ARE PLEASED TO BE ASSOCIATED WITH

THE 50TH ANNIVERSARY OF THE D-DAY LANDINGS

"WE WILL REMEMBER THEM"

THE INFANTRY

D-Day soldiers will have no difficulty in recognising

the role of the modern infantry:

To close with and destroy the enemy by both day and

night, over all terrain and in all weathers.

With modern technology the infantry can now engage an

enemy and kill him from 2,000 metres and beyond, yet the basic

requirement to engage in close quarter combat remains, as was

shown in the Falklands War in 1982 and the Gulf War in 1991.

Additionally the modern soldier is also placed in environments that demand tact, self control and moral courage when dealing with civilians in counter terrorism situations and the protection of the weak in humanitarian aid operations.

Such a diverse spectrum of operations - from all-out war to smaller conflicts and finally to military activities in peace-demands the flexibility of mind and organization that has led to the infantry being the most versatile combat arm in the Army today.

This versatility is one of mind, body, equipment and procedures and is demonstrated by the number of different types of infantry battalions ranging from armoured infantry equipped with the Warrior Infantry Fighting Vehicle, to light role battalions equipped with wheeled vehicles: from parachute and airborne battalions, an asset that can be moved from theatre to theatre and offering strategic mobility ,to battalions trained in jungle operations in Belize and Brunei. The modern infantryman soon discovers that he must be a master of a number of roles so that he can be sent from a

A Warrier Infantry Combat Vehicle painted in UN colours operating in Bosnia. This vehicle gave British forces in Bosnia an edge over all other contingents. It is highly mobile, heavily armoured and packs the punch of a 30mm Raden canon.

mechanised battalion equipped with the Saxon armoured personnel carrier to an operational tour in Northern Ireland where counter-terrorism operations demand the ability to patrol on foot and in vehicles, to operate with helicopters and to use sophisticated surveillance and communication equipment.

THE INFANTRY SOLDIER

However many types of battalions we have, the basic building block is the individual infantryman. He is equipped with the SA80 Individual Weapon or the Light Support Weapon machine gun. He is armed with a bayonet and grenades, both thrown by hand and projected from the rifle. He is protected from surveillance by modern camouflaged uniforms that offer a shield from visual and image intensification devices and from nuclear, biological and chemical attack by a protective suit and respirator. He has the ability to acquire and engage targets with magnified optical sights by both day, using the Sight Unit Small Arms Trilux (SUSAT) and night by using the Common Weapon Sight. Through his team commander the individual soldier has the means to communicate that enables him to react quickly to a change in situation . He can survive for several days with what he can carry on his webbing and he can strip this down to light order when he is required to close with and destroy the enemy. A rifleman will take his part as a member of a four man fire team equipped with three Individual Weapons and one Light Support Weapon: there are two fire teams per section, three sections in a rifle platoon and three platoons in a rifle company.

THE BATTALION

To support the rifle companies each battalion has its heavier weapons. The 81mm mortar gives the commanding officer his own integral fire support enabling targets out to 5,800 metres to be engaged. The mortar can be man-packed, transported in a vehicle or operated from an Armoured Fighting Vehicle series 432. Whilst the 81mm mortar is a battalion asset each rifle platoon has a 51mm system capable of firing high explosive, smoke and illumination rounds up to 800 metres.

The man-portable anti-tank capability is provided by the throw away 94mm Light Anit-Tank Weapon, six of which are carried in each rifle section and which is capable of defeating enemy vehicles out to 500 metres by day and night. At the battalion level a medium rang anti-tank missile - Milan - is provided which is capable of destroying targets out to 1,950 metres and has a thermal imaging sight that enables the firer to engage targets by night as by day and gives him the ability to see through battlefield obscuration such as smoke and fog. The Milan is operated by the anti-tank platoon, the size of which varies according to the type of battalion from 28 soldiers manning six firing posts in a light role battalion, through 24 posts in armoured infantry, parachute and airborne battalions to 113 soldiers manning 42 posts in an airmobile battalion.

The medium machine gun support for the battalion is provided by the medium machine gun platoon manning the 7.62mm General Purpose Machine Gun in the sustained fire role mounted on a tripod. This has an effective range out to 1,800 metres and can be fired by day or night either using direct or indirect fire control.

These support elements, 81mm Mortar, Milan and the Medium Machine gun are normally found in the support company of a battalion. However, on operations, elements will be grouped to the three rifle companies. Whilst all the operators of this equipment are specialists they are also required to maintain their normal infantry skills of fitness, shooting, NBC, map-reading, signals and fieldcraft thereby enabling them to change role at a moment's notice.

The battalion's ability to react quickly to orders and to changes in situations is a direct result of their communications. The signals platoon provides the commanding officer with the means to communicate his intentions and orders his companies and specialist platoons by radio, or, in defensive positions, also by land-line or wire. These communication assets, that now include the use of date entry devices for the rapid transmission of orders and reports, when combined with the ability of fast-moving vehicles such as Warrior to know exactly where they are using the Satellite Global Positioning System, provides a huge increase in the flexibility of the infantry.

An 81mm mortar crew loading a bomb into the mortar tube. Mortars give the infantry the mobility to hit back at unseen targets up to 8km away. Their essential design has changed little since the second World War, though their accuracy ,lethality and range has improved dramatically.

The eyes and ears of the commanding officer remain his reconnaissance platoon which is equipped with the Scimitar Armoured Fighting Vehicle or Land-Rovers. They have equipment that enables them to see by night as by day using the Spyglass Thermal Imager, which can be mounted with a Laser Range Finder, and an Image Intensifier night sight on the Scimitar. When dismounted they operate as normal infantry and are similarly equipped. They use remote sensors to detect the enemy in dead ground and can call on the battalion's integral fire support by radio.

In addition to these fighting assets each battalion has its own combat support based on A and B Echelons through which the fighting soldiers gain their re-supplies of ammunition, food and Petrol Oil and Lubricants (POL). The mechanical transport platoon ensures that the combat supplies are moved quickly and efficiently and the regimental medical assistants ensure that casualties are moved back as painlessly as possible.

Whilst the assault pioneers in most battalions are double-hatted, that is they fulfil their normal infantry section work until called upon to carry out specialist tasks, they do give the commanding officer his own integral light engineering support. The range of power tools that they operate is fast making them an invaluable asset in peacetime emergency

operations as well as in general war. They operate mechanical handling equipment such as the Light Wheeled Tractor that enables them to dig defensive positions or handle stores; they can operate power boats and supervise the building of the infantry bridge that enables rivers 44 m wide to be crossed.

The commanding officer commands his battalion from his tactical headquarters supported by his operations officer and radio operators. This may be a Warrior or Saxon Command Vehicle, a Land-Rover or on foot. He will have at his main headquarters his second-in-command who will control the running of the battle supported by the mortar, anti-tank and signals platoon commanders as well as advisers from the artillery and other supporting organizations.

Therefore an infantry battalion, irrespective of the specific task it is given, is organized with three rifle companies of three platoons each; a support company having mortar, anti-tank, medium machine gun and reconnaissance platoons, a headquarters company giving it the ability to communicate and sustain itself and finally a headquarters that enables the commanding officer to command and control his battalion. All the functions are carried out by infantry whether they be a rifleman, guided missile operator, radio operator, vehicle crew, assault pioneer, surveillance device or support weapon operator.

MOBILITY

The mobility of the infantry varies from the parachute and airborne battalions with strategic but poor tactical mobility to light battalions that move by wheeled vehicles. When in a theatre the airmobile battalion, transported by helicopter, has the greatest operational mobility, while the armoured infantry battalions combine the most effective integral firepower with the greatest tactical mobility. All battalions can be moved by sea to new theatres of operations and the fact that a battalion has its own fire support, reconnaissance, anti-tank and ground-holding capability provides a flexible and versatile integrated fighting unit for rapid deployment in times of crisis. This versatility has been demonstrated on operations over the past 12 years in the Falkland Islands, The Gulf, Northern Ireland and Bosnia. Additionally, battalions are continually training for war in the Arctic and the jungle as well as for helicopter and airborne operations.

The Warrior Infantry Combat vehicle was the mainstay of the Infantry during the Gulf War. Its mobility and high speed enabled it to keep up with the Challenger tank and provide the essential infantry support needed by British armoured forces.

DISMOUNTED INFANTRY

The Falklands Campaign was a dismounted infantry war where the ability of trained infantry soldiers to move across hostile terrain, both in the climatic and tactical sense, was fully demonstrated. The traditional infantry role was fulfilled by the 2nd and 3rd Battalions The Parachute Regiment and the 1st Battalion Scots Guards in their attacks on Goose Green, Wireless Ridge, Mount Longdon and Mount Tumbledown. Conducted at night the battalions fought hand-to-hand for hours against Argentinian prepared positions and prevailed. Indeed, the requirement of infantry commanders to lead from the front and on foot, even in the modern era, was shown in the Battles of Goose Green and Mount Longdon when Lieutenant Colonel Herbert 'H' Jones and Sergeant Ian McKay both won Victoria Crosses posthumously for their bravery.

ARMOURED INFANTRY

The Gulf War of 1991 demonstrated that this traditional foot-slogging style of infantry warfare is now augmented by sophisticated vehicles that are not just armoured taxis but also potent fighting machines. The introduction of the Warrior Infantry Fighting Vehicle gives the infantry section, platoon and company commanders a number of what had previously been considered Armoured Corps tasks. At each level of command the number of manoeuvre units that can be deployed has been doubled since the Warrior, with a dedicated crew of three men, can operate in support of dismounted infantry or independently to the flank, to the rear, forward as part of a screen, or as a mobile reserve especially suited to anti-desant operations. Infantry commanders must therefore master mounted as well as dismounted tactics and communications, individual as well as collective Nuclear Biological and Chemical warfare protection and crew-served as well as individual weapon-handling and gunnery skills.

The Warrior, equipped with the Rarden 30mm cannon, is capable of engaging targets using armour-piercing discarding sabots or high explosive at battle ranges of 1,500 metres. It also has a coaxial 7.62mm chain gun mounted with the cannon. The Rarden cannon is not new to the infantry as it is also fitted to the Scimitar vehicle found in the reconnaissance platoon. An armoured infantry battalion, equipped with 57 Warriors retains the fire support provided by The Milan anti-tank guided missile, mounted in Warrior, and the 81mm Mortar mounted in the Armoured Fighting Vehicle 432 Armoured Personnel Carrier, thereby giving the commanding officer a mobile indirect fire capability.

The Warrior, with a maximum sustained speed of 80 kph, proved its worth in the Gulf War when the First Battalions of the Royal Scots and the Staffordshire Regiments, plus the Third Battalion, the Royal Regiment Fusiliers, all equipped with Warrior, took their place in the 4th and 7th Armoured brigades alongside the Royal Armoured Corps Challenger main battle tank. The speed of manoeuvre of these Brigades was a direct result of the speed of both vehicles, the skill of their crews and the quick thinking of their commanders. This speed and expertise was honed by a series of field training exercises in the desert prior to the operation, however the basis was a sophisticated training package particularly for the gunners and commanders of the Warrior vehicles. A desk top trainer is used for initial Warrior gunnery training and subsequently a platoon trainer allows armoured infantry platoons to practice advanced gunnery skills using simulators before deploying to open ranges. Whilst there is great emphasis on gunnery skills, commanders are well aware that dismounted skills must also be maintained.

The introduction of the Warrior has given commanders far greater flexibility with the combination of increased firepower, mobility and protection being the key to the vehicle's success. Warrior's optical systems and increased capability removed the total dependence that the infantry once had on their armoured counterparts for intimate support whilst approaching the objective and during the assault, fight-through and exploitation phases of a battle. In defence the combination of firepower and mobility enables the battle group commander to deploy Warrior with tanks to form a mobile reserve.

In war, armoured infantry will almost always operate as part of an all-arms grouping or formation whose primary role will be the destruction of the enemy. Within this grouping the role of the armoured infantry will be to close with the enemy and assist in his destruction often with the requirement to clear, control and if necessary hold ground. Implicit in this role are the following tasks:-

●The intimate support of armour to maintain or restore armoured mobility;

●The destruction of infantry and light armoured vehicles with Warrior's cannon and tanks with the Milan and Light Anti-Tank systems;

●The seizing, controlling and if necessary the holding of ground;

●The breaching and crossing of obstacles and establishing bridgeheads and playing a leading part in fighting in built up areas and woods and forests.

MECHANISED BATTALIONS

The Saxon vehicle is a four-wheeled Armoured Personnel Carrier providing protected mobility for four Infantry battalions which are called mechanised battalions each one of which is equipped with 64 Saxon vehicles. Its armour provides the infantry with a high degree of crew protection against shell splinters, small arms ammunition and blast mines enabling a commander to re-deploy his infantry without the need for low-loaders or trains to move battalions around a theatre of operations.

The tasks for the mechanised battalions are the same as those that light role battalions might be given and include defence against penetration by enemy armour by denying the passage of defiles and centres of communications; the provision of a defensive framework in depth around which mobile armoured elements of a force can operate; the protection of vital installations, routes and communication centres; the provision of demolition guards; the defence of urban areas; and counter-insurgency and internal security operations.

AIRMOBILE INFANTRY

The tactical mobility provided by Warrior and Saxon vehicles is complimented by the airmobile infantry battalions: that is those battalions that use support helicopters for operational movement. The value of an airmobile battalion is its ability to move rapidly by air, at short notice and to deploy a potent anti-tank capability as each battalion is equipped with 42 Milan Anti-Tank Guided Weapons.

An extensive range of vehicles is used by an airmobile battalion. This includes the motor-cycle, the six wheeled Supacat All Terrain Mobile Platform, the Ground Mobile Weapon Platform and Land-Rovers.

The airmobile role is one of extreme contrasts: preparation for a move from a staging area, the organization of rapid movement by helicopter and then on foot or by a small number of light vehicles air-lifted forward, demand extreme flexibility of thought and action as well as a breadth of vision by commanders at all levels.

PARACHUTE AND AIRBORNE BATTALIONS

Parachute and airborne battalions must be capable of moving at short notice anywhere in the world by air to conduct a range of operations. These operations include the key requirement to conduct a direct parachute assault either independently of co-ordinated with a tactical airland assault operation. To achieve this and exploit fully the surprise which can be achieved by both parachute and airland assault there is a requirement for strategic and tactical mobility and strike power within the airborne force. Mobility and firepower are finely balanced however, with the requirement for relative lightness, particularly during the initial phases of an airborne operation where much is man-packed and vehicles are restricted by the air flow phase. All parachute and airborne battalions can land with 24 Milan firing posts providing them with a significant anti-tank capability. Both in this battalion and all others eight men will be trained snipers capable of engaging targets using the 7.62mm Sniper Rifle.

LIGHT ROLE BATTALIONS

The light role battalion has sufficient wheeled vehicles to lift the battalion complete. However a dismounted battalion, suitably trained and acclimatized can negotiate almost any type of terrain and would normally take its support weapons with it. In close and difficult country the speed and endurance of the marching soldier will govern the mobility achieved thereby reinforcing the importance of physical fitness in all battalions.

The light role battalion is designed to operate with support from other arms and services in a regional war and other conflicts against enemy regular and irregular forces equipped with modern conventional weapons. It is also capable of undertaking operations in general war. The battalions are air-portable and trained to make full use of helicopters and fixed-wing aircraft for tactical mobility and logistic support.

ACE MOBILE FORCE (LAND) BATTALION

One further battalion is allocated to the Allied Commander's Europe (ACE) Mobile Force (Land) commitment. This battalion trains in Arctic Warfare where it must learn the new skills of fighting and surviving in the Arctic including the requirement to use the BV 206 over-snow vehicle. All soldiers in the battalion learn how to ski and how to employ support weapons in the Arctic and to use support helicopters for re-supply and casualty evacuation.

JUNGLE OPERATIONS

Whilst one battalion is trained in Arctic Warfare all battalions could expect to send soldiers to train in jungle operations at the Training Centre in Brunei and also to participate in operations in Belize. Whilst the basic infantry skills such as navigation, fieldcraft, patrolling and shooting are all vital, new skills such as jungle survival, tracking, booby-trap awareness, close-target reconnaissance, harbouring, river crossing techniques and helicopter drills have to be acquired by soldiers leaving to operate in the jungle.

NORTHERN IRELAND

Battalions operate in Northern Ireland where their normal infantry skills are tested to the full and for which a sophisticated training package has been developed concentrating on internal security duties both in urban and rural environments. This ensures that before a battalion deploys new procedures, weapons and equipment have all to be mastered.

The role of the infantry in Northern Ireland is to support the Royal Ulster Constabulary in the defeat of terrorism as part of the Government's strategy to restore normality to the Province. This role demands that soldiers not only deal with terrorist incidents, but also, and most importantly, develop good relations with the local communities in order to maintain public support. An understanding of the political situation and the many legal aspects of operating in Northern Ireland is vital. Junior commanders have a great deal of operational responsibility. Detailed briefings and orders, motivation, self discipline and morale, as well as the traditional infantry skills are all thoroughly tested in a challenging operational environment.

UN OPERATIONS

The experience of Northern Ireland was useful when the infantry formed a significant part of the UK contribution to Bosnia. An armoured infantry battalion is deployed to Central Bosnia with the role of supporting the United Nations High Commission for Refugees in the distribution of humanitarian aid. This demands impartiality, fairness and integrity in dealing with all sides. Warriors are used extensively to protect the convoys yet the critical part of the success of the operation is the versatility of individual soldiers when dealing with refugees, protagonists and the media. The tenacity and good humour of soldiers, combined with constant vigilance have ensured that the British contribution to the UN operations is well respected.

SUMMARY

The infantry remains the largest element in the modern British Army and must master a wide variety of skills, be prepared to operate in a wide range of environments and in varying scales of conflict from activities in peace through global police actions, and skirmishes to all-out war; and be able to operate sophisticated and technically-advanced vehicles and equipment.

An infantryman must be physically fit, mentally tough, confident in his own and his comrade's abilities, and versatile. The intervening years since D-Day have reinforced the reputation of the infantry so proudly demonstrated on the beaches of Normandy and elsewhere.

Modern Infantrymen are required to fight a 24 hour battle. The Spy Glass Thermal Imager which enhances the heat signal given off by both men and equipment enables these infantrymen to detect enemy movement at night and in adverse weather conditions.

THE FUTURE

J ust as the Armed Forces of the Crown have changed dramatically in the 50 years since D-Day so too will they have to change as they face the future. The Armed Forces of the future will face different challenges and different enemies. They will continue to need high quality individuals and sophisticated equipment in order to do the job. Typical of the needs of the armed forces of the 21st Century are;

Above
The AH-64 Apache Helicopter Gun Ship equipped with the chin-mounted 30mm chain gun and hellfire pods outboard of the fuselage.

Left
The European fighter aircraft (EFA) will be the backbone of the Royal Air Force well into the 21st Century. It's maiden flight took place in Germany on the 27th March 1994. It is expected to be in service with the Royal Air Force is the late 1990's.
Below
The Duke Class Type 23 Anti-Submarine Warfare Frigate will be the mainstay of the Royal Navy for the next several decades.

Perkins Powerpacks.
Performance where you need it most.

From the searing heat of the desert to the freezing temperatures of Central Europe, Perkins diesel engines, transmissions and fully integrated Powerpacks constantly deliver out-standing performance.

Their mobility in these extreme conditions underlines their reputation as the driving force behind the world's most successful military fighting vehicles.

For more information on our comprehensive range of battle proven engines, transmissions and Powerpacks contact Perkins Defence Systems at Perkins Engines (Shrewsbury) Ltd. Lancaster Road, Shrewsbury, SY1 4DP, England. Tel: 44 (0) 743-212000. Fax: 44 (0) 743-212701.

Perkins

A business of Varity Corporation. VARITY